Tithing: Reviewing Scripture in Context

An RS teacher's Investigation of Bible Evidence and Historical Sources

Karsten Wille

DEDICATION

I would like to dedicate this book to my beautiful wife Michelle, my son Dietrich and my daughter Monet-Grace.

CONTENTS

ACKNOWLEDGMENTS

Thank you to Dr. Patrick Businge and his wife Julian Businge for encouraging me to use my knowledge of scripture to continue educating people in God's word. A special thanks to my mother for helping me with the editing.

PREFACE

This book aims to analyse scripture in the context of all Bible books relating to tithing, also gathering an insight into the early characters this topic relies heavily upon. Tithing is mentioned many times in the Bible and many theories have developed over time regarding this subject, especially concerning the expressed need of giving a tenth of one's income in the New Testament Church. This subject has divided many with a focus on the Law and freewill giving. On the one hand you will have those who will push for Malachi 3:10 with all their conviction and energy, and on the reverse side of the coin, will be the Christian who makes an important distinction between what belonged to the law in the Old Testament and what adheres to grace in the New Testament.

My intention is to delve into scripture, commenting on the customs and cultures of the times they were written and the audiences they were meant to capture. Scripture is only useful if we rightly divide the word of truth, which is consequently only possible if we study ourselves approved. (2 Timothy 2:15) This can only be done by mainly digging heavily into the Old Testament and gaining an idea of ancient customs and Judaic culture and the laws commanded by God at that time. Equally important will be the definition of tithing and what was actually required of Israel. Modern day replacement theology has taken on the idea of the literal replacement of the Jewish people favoured by God and bound by the law, or even pre-law statute, putting the Body of Christ in their place, inclusive of the requirement of tithing. The New Testament has very little to say on the matter and any scripture evidence will also be put into context, inclusive of New Testament giving and what was actually put into practice by the Apostles. Context is crucial when dealing with God's word and no quote says it better than by Dr. Ben Witherington:

"A Text without a context is just a pretext for what we want it to mean..." (*Witherington 2009* p 41)

It is very clear that modern day Evangelical Churches have a very keen interest to contextualize scripture to include the law of tithing, as the accumulation of ten percent from each congregant does spell the backbone and foundation of giving for many, thus financially supporting the daily running of a Church or ministry. As a matter of fact, you will be hard pressed to find an evangelical church that does not uphold this principle. For some churches it has actually become a prerequisite for membership. All scriptures in the Bible making mention of the tithe will be quoted and historically contextualized. I will also be reviewing scriptural accounts that frequently will be used to support the principle of tithing or even the emphasis of giving all. The Apostle Paul will feature heavily as he wrote most of the epistles in the New Testament. I will also investigate whether the philosophy of the tithe was adhered to by the early church; furthermore, explore historical records as to when this idea gained favour by the clergy and state.

I will summarize all the main points of the study of scripture and context, then finalize the findings in easy to navigate bullet points to form an overview, narrowing evidence into a systematic review. A clear picture of the subject will arise, whereby you can determine your own conclusions regarding this topic.

The beginning of this book will unfold with your own involvement. I would like you to consider the famous church Fathers and theologians over the next couple of pages and decide what they all have in common. The reflection following the brief character studies will confirm your analysis.

Tithing: Reviewing Scripture in Context

Early Church Fathers and Theologians

St Irenaeus (130 - 202)

Irenaeus was born of Greek parents, a leading Christian theologian of the 2nd century, Bishop of Lyon and clearly formulated church doctrine by which he took a strong stance against emerging Gnosticism, resisting all heresy and defining orthodox belief. He did much to validate both Testaments in the Bible during a time of confusion and upheaval. (Encyclopedia Britannica). He wrote many sacred writings with untold volumes including 'Against Heresies' in the year 180 AD.

Concerning tithing in his book 'Against Heresies' he writes:

"And for this reason did the Lord, instead of that [commandment], `You shall not commit adultery,' forbid even concupiscence; and instead of that which runs thus,

7

`You shall not kill,' He prohibited anger; and instead of the law enjoining the giving of **tithes**, to share all our possessions with the poor; and not to love our neighbors only, but even our enemies; and not merely to be liberal givers and bestowers, but even that we should present a gratuitous gift to those who take away our goods"* (**Book 4 chapter 13**)

*"And the class of oblations in general has not been set aside; for there were both oblations there [among the Jews], and there are oblations here [among the Christians]. Sacrifices there were among the people; sacrifices there are, too, in the Church: but the species alone has been changed, inasmuch as the offering is now made, not by slaves, but by freemen. For the Lord is [ever] one and the same; but the character of a servile oblation is peculiar [to itself], as is also that of freemen, in order that, by the very oblations, the indication of liberty may be set forth. For with Him there is nothing purposeless, nor without signification, nor without design. And for this reason they (the Jews) had indeed the **tithes** of their goods consecrated to Him, but those who have received liberty set aside all their possessions for the Lord's purposes, bestowing joyfully and freely not the less valuable portions of their property, since they have the hope of better things [hereafter]; as that poor widow acted who cast all her living into the treasury of God'.* **Irenaeus, Against Heresies, Chapter 18, Concerning Sacrifices and Oblations, and Those Who Truly Offer Them; 180 AD**

John Wycliffe (1330-1384)

John Wycliffe is known as an early English protestant reformer and is famous for being one of the first people to translate the Bible into the English language. He was a theologian, philosopher and one of the people blazing a path for the Protestant reformation way ahead of its time. **(Encyclopedia Britannica)**

Concerning tithing, he writes:

*"Why curates are so severe in exacting **tithes**, since Christ and his apostles took no **tithes**, as men do now; neither paid them, nor even spoke of them, either in the Gospel or the Epistles, which are the perfect law of freedom and grace. But Christ lived on the alms of holy women, as the Gospel telleth ; and the apostles lived sometimes by the labor of their hands, and sometimes took a poor livelihood and clothing, given of free will and devotion by the people, without asking or constraining." " Paul proved that priests, preaching truly the gospel, should live by the gospel, and said naught of **tithes**. Certainly **tithes** were due to priests in the Old Law — but it is*

not so now, in the law of grace."

John Wycliffe, *Tracts and Treatises of John de Wycliffe, D.D. with Selections and Translations from his Manuscripts, and Latin Works.* Edited for The Wycliffe Society, with an Introductory Memoir, by the Rev. Robert Vaughan, D.D. (London: Blackburn and Pardon, 1845)

Erasmus *(1466-1536)*

Erasmus was known as the greatest scholar of the Northern Renaissance and editor of the New Testament. Erasmus was a forerunner for the historical-critical study of the past, especially in his studies of the Greek New Testament and the Church Fathers. He supported both the Protestant Reformation and the Catholic Counter Reformation. **(Encyclopedia Britannica)**

Concerning tithing, he writes:

"And yet, disgusting as it is to see Christian princes in this field more inhuman than pagan tyrants ever were, yet this is a little less outrageous than the fact that among our priests also, in whose eyes all money ought to be quite worthless and whose duty it is freely to share the endowments they have so freely

*received, everything has its price, nothing is free. Think of the storms they raise over those famous **tithes** of theirs, how hatefully they oppress wretched common people! You cannot be baptized, which means that you cannot become a Christian unless you pay cash; such are the splendid auspices under which you enter the portals of the Church.*"

"The Adages of Erasmus" p.122, 1946; Translation by William Barker, University of Toronto press.

Martin Luther (1483-1546)

Martin Luther was responsible for standing against the Catholic Church and starting the protestant reformation. His teaching emphasized the authority of God's word over the authority of the Catholic Church; furthermore the belief that we are saved by Grace and not by works. He also made the very brave move of translating the Bible into German. He is credited with being one of the most influential figures in Christendom in the last millennium, without whom we would not have had a Church split or Protestantism as we know it today. **(Encyclopedia Britannica)**

Concerning tithing, he writes: *'But the other commandments of Moses, which are not [Implanted in all men] by nature, the Gentiles do not hold. Nor do these pertain to the Gentiles, such as the tithe'.*

'How Christians should regard Moses', p139, August 27, 1525.

John Wesley (1703-1791)

John Wesley was an English theologian and evangelist. He was the founder of a revival movement within the Church of England, which gave birth to the Methodist Church.

(Photo Credit: Encyclopedia Britannica)

Concerning the tithe, he writes: *'Do not stint yourself, like a Jew rather than a Christian, to this or that proportion. "Render unto God," not a **tenth**, not a third, not half, but all that is God's, be it more or less; by employing all on yourself, your household, the household of faith, and all mankind, in such a manner, that you may give a good account of your stewardship when ye can be no longer stewards...'*

Sermon 'The Use of Money'. Methodist Publication. May 17th 2011, John Meunier

Charles Spurgeon (1834-1892)

Charles Spurgeon was an Englishman and Particular Baptist Preacher with fame and recognition across many denominations. His oral skill earned him the title as 'Prince of Preachers', standing strong against any form of liberalism creeping its way into the Body of Christ.

(Photo Credit: Oneplace)

His view on the subject of tithing was as follows:

*'Tis ridiculous to say the **tithes** are God's part, and therefore the clergy must have them; why, so they are if the layman has them. 'Tis as if one of my Lady Kent's maids should be sweeping this room, and another of them should come and take away the broom, and tell for a reason why she should part with it, 'tis my lady's broom; as if it were not my lady's broom which of them so ever had it.: Table Talk of John Selden*

Spurgeon, Charles. Entry for 'Tithes'. Charles Spurgeon's Illustration Collection, 1870.

Reflection on Church Fathers and Theologians

Judging by these church Fathers and theologians to name but a few, you will have discovered that all of them did not pertain favourably to the concept of tithing in the New Testament Church. They all would have followed and encouraged free will offerings in a way that congregants would have been giving to the church in keeping with their own income, personal finances and responsibilities. This ignites the very important question – what is the tithe? The answer to this question is more complex than the giving of a simple explanation, an explanation which almost all of us would never have received in church, during the time of the collection in the service or for better words, referred to as 'tithes and offerings'. Most people are unlikely to know the difference.

What is the tithe?

Hodder and Stoughton illustrated Bible Dictionary defines the tithe as the following:

The practice of giving a tenth of one's income or property as an offering to God. The custom of paying a tithe was an ancient practice found among many nations of the ancient world.

The practice of giving a tenth of income or property extends into Hebrew history before the time of the Mosaic Law. The first recorded instance of tithing in the Bible occurs in Genesis 14:17-20. After returning from rescuing Lot and defeating his enemies, Abraham met Melchizedek, 'the King of Salem' and 'priest of God most high'. The text states simply that Abraham gave Melchizedek a tithe of all the goods he had obtained in battle. The author of the book of Hebrews, in recounting this episode, considered the Levitical priests who descended from Abraham and who appeared centuries later as having paid tithes to Melchizedek through Abraham (Heb. 7:1-10). There is no recorded demand for a tenth. Neither an explanation given about why Abraham gave a tithe to Melchizedek. Jacob also, long before the law of Moses, promised that he would give to the Lord a tenth of all he received (Gen 28:22). The Law of Moses prescribed tithing in some detail. Leviticus 27:30-32 stated that the tithe of the land would include the seed of the land and the fruit of the tree.

In the New Testament the words tithe and tithing appear only eight times (Matt 23:23; Luke 11:42; 18:12; Heb. 7:5-6,8-9) All these passages refer to Old Testament usage and to Jewish practice. Nowhere does the New Testament expressly command Christians to tithe. However, as believers we are to be generous in sharing our material possessions with the poor and for the support of Christian ministry. Christ himself is our model in giving. Giving is to be voluntary, willing, cheerful, and given in the light of our accountability to God. Giving should be systematic and by no means limited to a tithe of our incomes. We recognize that all we have is from God. We are called to be faithful stewards of all our possessions (Rom. 14:12; 1 Cor.9:3-14; 16:1-3; 2 Cor. 8-9). **(Hodder and Stoughton Illustrated Bible Dictionary).**

Hodder and Stoughton's definition does set the record straight as to what the tithe was, furthermore is very detailed concerning the appearance of the word and usage of the word in the New Testament and the requirement of giving set out in the epistles, not relating to any type of tithe by law or necessity of a given percentage.

The Zondervan Bible Dictionary also lets us know more as to what resources were tithed:

'Tithe (tenth), 10th part of one's income set aside for a specific use, to the government or ecclesiastics. Its origin is unknown, but it goes back far beyond the time of Moses, and it was practised in lands from Babylonia to Rome. Abraham gave tithes to Melchizedek (Gen 14:20; Heb. 7:2, 6); Jacob promised tithes to God (Gen. 28:22); Mosaic law required tithing of all **produce of land and herds** *(Lev, 27:30-33); use for support of Levites and priests (Num. 18. 21-32); additional tithes may have been required at certain times (Deut. 12:5-18; 14:22-29); there were penalties for cheating in tithing (Lev. 27:31; Deut. 26; 13-15). Pharisees tithed even* **herbs** *Matt. 22:23; Luke 11:42).* **(Zondervan Bible Dictionary)**

In this Bible dictionary definition, we can also see that the tithe consisted of not just a 10th, but in some cases and at certain times considerably more. The Mosaic Law tithe was also always paid in the form of **produce of the Land** or by

herds of cattle, in other words '**FOOD**'! I will explain more about the different types of tithes and percentages required later on in this book, but it is important that it is understood that the 'tithe', did not consist of money, although money and currency was already in use and operation in Genesis. We only have one instance in scripture when these food items could be converted into money for the purpose of paying the tithe (Deut. 14:25-27). Furthermore, this tithe was consumed and eaten by the person tithing, without ignoring the Levites who were also present. I will provide a more detailed description relating to this later on in this book.

Something important to note in both Dictionary definitions, is that the tithe was not simply a Jewish custom on behalf of a theocracy, but was also part of the ancient customs in all the regions of Mesopotamia and beyond, which is put in a time frame in the pre-law period. Since the Bible records the word tithe in the pre-law period, with notably two important characters who are Abraham and his grandson Jacob, it may be of value to do a character study on both of them, allowing us to explore the nature of the recording of the tithe.

Tithing: Reviewing Scripture in Context

Abraham and the Tithe

As we previously discovered, the first mention of the word tithe in the Bible is linked to Abraham. He was the patriarch and founding father of the Jewish race, Judaism and effectively the first Jew. He made a covenant with God and in the New Testament he is recorded as being God's friend, which is highly unusual (James 2:23). He is a character who scripture has the most to say about, as the appearance of his name is all over the Bible and listed more times than any other person. He is not just the Father of the Jews, but by faith he is the Father of the Gentiles as well, whereby we have all become children of Abraham (Galatians 3:7). There is little known about his early life, but the narrative starts with Abram, when he is in his 70s. God calls him out of his father's household, to distance himself from his kin folk, in order for God to talk to him and establish a covenant with him. He would have followed the customs of the time and lived amongst pagan worshippers of idols in Ur and Haran. These customs also included the paying of a tax, usually an approximation of a 10th as a form of tribute to the King or ambassador.

Abraham had spent a period of time in Egypt and through God's favor obtained a tremendous amount of wealth that under the circumstances he did not deserve. Nowhere is it recorded that he tithed any of this (these were now his possessions). He left with sheep, goats, servants and cattle, as well as silver and gold. Later due to a disagreement with his nephew Lot, the both agreed to separate, with Lot choosing the Fertile Crescent in the Jordan Valley, whereas Abraham stayed in the land of Canaan. Lot settled in the valley and camped near Sodom, whose people were wicked and sinned against the Lord.

As life continued we have an extraordinary event, in that Lot thinking he had made a good deal by picking the most fertile land, found himself in grievous danger and was dragged off, including all the possessions of the Kings of Sodom and Gomorrah. Abram, then took it upon himself to rally his 318 trained servants to rescue his extended family. The account in Genesis 14:1-24 is recorded as follows:

Lot's Captivity and Rescue

14 And it came to pass in the days of Amraphel king of Shinar, Arioch king of Ellasar, Chedorlaomer king of Elam, and Tidal king of [a] nations, ² that they made war with Bera king of Sodom, Birsha king of Gomorrah, Shinab king of Admah, Shemeber king of Zeboiim, and the king of Bela (that is, Zoar). ³ All these joined together in the Valley of Siddim (that is, the Salt Sea). ⁴ Twelve years they served Chedorlaomer, and in the thirteenth year they rebelled.

⁵ In the fourteenth year Chedorlaomer and the kings that were with him came and attacked the Rephaim in Ashteroth Karnaim, the Zuzim in Ham, the Emim in Shaveh Kiriathaim, ⁶ and the Horites in their mountain of Seir, as far as El Paran, which is by the wilderness. ⁷ Then they turned back and came to En Mishpat (that is, Kadesh), and attacked all the country of the Amalekites, and also the Amorites who dwelt in Hazezon Tamar.

⁸ And the king of Sodom, the king of Gomorrah, the king of Admah, the king of Zeboiim, and the king of Bela (that is, Zoar) went out and joined together in battle in the Valley of Siddim ⁹ against Chedorlaomer king of Elam, Tidal king of [b] nations, Amraphel king of Shinar, and Arioch king of Ellasar—four kings against five. ¹⁰ Now the Valley of Siddim was full of asphalt pits; and the kings of Sodom and Gomorrah fled; some fell there, and the remainder fled to the mountains. [11] Then they took all the goods of Sodom and Gomorrah, and all their provisions, and went their way. [12] They also took Lot, Abram's brother's son who dwelt in Sodom, and his goods, and departed.

[13] Then one who had escaped came and told Abram the Hebrew, for he dwelt by [a]the terebinth trees of Mamre the Amorite, brother of Eshcol and brother of Aner; and they were allies with Abram. [14] Now when Abram heard that his brother was taken captive, he armed his three hundred and eighteen trained servants who were born in his own house, and went in pursuit as far as Dan. [15] He divided his forces against them by night, and he and his servants attacked them and pursued them as far as Hobah, which is [b]north of Damascus. [16] So he brought back all the goods, and also brought back his brother Lot and his goods, as well as the women and the people.

[17] And the king of Sodom went out to meet him at the Valley of Shaveh (that is, the King's Valley), after his return from the [c]defeat of Chedorlaomer and the kings who were with him.

Abram and Melchizedek

[18] Then Melchizedek king of Salem brought out bread and wine; he was the priest of God Most High. [19] And he blessed him and said:

"Blessed be Abram of God Most High,
Possessor of heaven and earth;
[20] And blessed be God Most High,
Who has delivered your enemies into your hand."

And he gave him [d]a tithe of all.

[21] Now the king of Sodom said to Abram, "Give me the

[a]*persons, and take the goods for yourself."*

[22] *But Abram said to the king of Sodom, "I have raised my hand to the LORD, God Most High, the Possessor of heaven and earth,* [23] *that I will take nothing, from a thread to a sandal strap, and that I will not take anything that is yours, lest you should say, 'I have made Abram rich'—* [24] *except only what the young men have eaten, and the portion of the men who went with me: Aner, Eshcol, and Mamre; let them take their portion."* **Genesis 14:1-24**

This is the recording of the first tithe in the Bible. It is also frequently used by those who support the concept of the tithe, that paying a tenth is pre-law and therefore is some kind of eternal moral principle of giving one must follow. This argument maintains that the tithe is therefore not just bound by the Mosaic Law, but rather presented as a nature of spiritual foundation for Biblical financial sowing and reaping. On a first light read, it can be seen how this could be an eternal moral principle, however on closer inspection, a number of very important questions start to arise.

The first question that comes to mind concerns the ownership of the spoils of war that were given as a tribute or tithe to Melchizedek. It is very clear in the passage that anything pertaining to giving here is not linked to any form of ownership on behalf of Abram. The only thing relating to Abram in this instance, is the fact that he is rescuing his family relation Lot. In order for a person to tithe, they must offer a 10th of what belongs to them, however what is presented is tribute from spoils of war belonging to the King of Sodom. The King of Sodom decided that he would be happy enough having his people returned to him and that if Abram wanted, he could take all the goods for himself, but Abram refuses any type of reward, not even a thread to a sandal strap. This may also indicate how Abraham felt about this King. He took only what his men had eaten, probably after working up a hunger, and that is the grand total. I would challenge anyone to use this example as an eternal moral principle for giving a tenth, especially if it is not from their own income. This could be likened to being employed by a company, and using company finances to pay the tithe. It is not a basis for any Church Doctrine of giving.

The second question which has to be answered is the mysterious nature of Melchizedek 'King of Salem'. If you are relying on the theory of Melchizedek as the personage of Jesus, a 'Christophany', or type of pre-incarnate Christ, then the evidence for this is in short supply. It is Melchizedek who feeds the hungry and weary men in the presence of the King of Sodom and it is the King of Sodom who offers them the goods in return for re-capturing all that was his. This links Melchizedek to the King of Sodom. This is a very curious union, being that the city of Sodom and Gomorrah are on God's hit list for destruction. We have a true 'Christophany', in (Genesis 18: 1-15), when Abraham is visited by three men, one of whom is referred to as the Lord. The Lord informs Sarah that she will have a child nine months later. In (Genesis 18: 16-33), it is then Abraham who is pleading with the Lord not to destroy Sodom and Gomorrah, dwindling down the number of the righteous to appease the Lord not to wipe out the cities. This is the second time Abraham is attempting to come to Lot's rescue as a result of his choices. One may view Melchizedek as a type of Christ, possibly prefiguring the ministry of the Lord, but we cannot put him in the personage as a pre-incarnate Christ with Abram presenting a tithe of what was not his, to form a basis for New Testament tithing. In Hebrews 7:3 concerning Milchizedek's lineage it is written that he was:

25

'without father, without mother, without genealogy, having neither beginning of days nor end of life, but made like the Son of God, remains a priest continually'. **Hebrews 7:3**

This however, does not affirm whether he was actually Jesus or figuratively a picture of the Levitical system to come. All that the passage in Hebrews confirms, is that Jesus was above Melchizedek and the Levitical priesthood. Had Melchizedek been Priest of the Most High, Genesis 14:18, then there would have been little point in Abraham's calling, if God already has a person in place to do the job. Russell E Kelly also points out, that the term 'Most High God', is unlikely to refer to Jehovah and may be the Canaanite God Baal:

'Melchizedek might have been identifying himself as a Semitic Canaanite by calling himself priest of 'El Elyon', 'Most High God'. As just mentioned, this reference, 'Most High God', was almost universally used by non-Hebrew Semitic people to designate their concept of 'Baal', or even his father 'El', the bull-god and father of the Canaanite pantheon'. (Kelly 2007 p 21)

A third very important discovery upon closer inspection of the text is the absence of a command. God is very clear with instructions and doesn't leave ambiguity to determine an outcome.

[10']This is My covenant which you shall keep, between Me and you and your descendants after you: Every male child among you shall be circumcised'. **Genesis 17:10**

Chapter 17 of Genesis starts with the need for Abraham's obedience in this situation, it cannot be misinterpreted. It was a principle that had to be kept under all costs. Circumcision was the law and a sign of covenant with Yahweh. Even later in Genesis 22:2 after Sodom and Gomorrah had been destroyed, God gives Abraham definitive instruction requiring obedience, which turned out to be a test in the offering of his only son.

²'Then He said, "Take now your son, your only son Isaac, whom you love, and go to the land of Moriah, and offer him there as a burnt offering on one of the mountains of which I shall tell you.' **Genesis 22:2**

Here we have the foreshadowing of what is due to take place at Calvary, when God chose to offer his only begotten son as an offering for all mankind. The act of Abraham had God's future redemptive plan written all over it. Even the appearance of a ram with its head stuck in the thicket was the perfect example of the provision of God and reward for obedience, so much so that Abraham called that place *'The Lord Provides',* **Genesis 22:14.**

The only conclusion we are likely to draw from the tithe Abraham offered to Melchizedek, is that he made a choice to do so, not compelled to do so by a clear instruction or command of the Lord. We also have no reference as to any verbal exchanges between Abraham and Melchizedek. This is why we lack the evidence to suggest that tithing is pre-Law and commanded by God as a universal eternal principle that should be followed to this day and neither are we encouraged to practice many of the customs or commandments God made to Abraham. There is no record in scripture that Abraham ever tithed again.

Tithing: Reviewing Scripture in Context

Jacob and the Tithe

When we refer to God in the Old Testament, we often refer to him either as 'The Great **I am**', or before the time of Moses as the God of **Abraham, Isaac** and **Jacob**. Abraham was the man who left his father's household to hear from God. Isaac was the man required to occupy his father's household. Jacob was the one known as not completely honest and was a 'twister'. In the previous chapter, we saw how God blessed Abraham, made him a person of tremendous wealth, and this blessing and favour with man was passed on to his son Isaac.

"And Isaac sowed in that land and reaped in the same year a hundredfold. The LORD blessed him, [13] and the man became rich, and gained more and more until he became very wealthy. [14] He had possessions of flocks and herds and many servants, so that the Philistines envied him. [15] (Now the Philistines had stopped and filled with earth all the wells that his father's servants had dug in the days of Abraham his father.) [16] And Abimelech said to Isaac, "Go away from us, for you are much mightier than we." **(Genesis 26:12-16)**

It is clear from the outset that God indeed did bless people with a rich heritage and with tremendous wealth, but was this due to a tithing philosophy? We know Abraham and Isaac built altars to the Lord as an act of worship and to temporarily atone for sin by sacrificing livestock. However, tithing as we know under the mosaic law was not practised as yet. *They acted as their own priests.* This is why we have no record of Isaac having tithed. Any concept of tithing to yourself or your own family has never had a basis in replacement theology and is clearly not encouraged in the New Testament Church.

To put the account of Jacob and the tithe into context, we first have to look at the background leading up to Jacob making a vow to God based on a tithe. Let us look at his family life first. When Isaac's wife Rebecca gave birth, she gave birth to a set of twins, both struggling with one another from the womb. They were called Esau and Jacob. As it can be with many families, parents sometimes pick their favourite child. In this case the twins were at odds with one another, Rebecca favouring her son Jacob who would dwell amongst the tents, but Isaac loved his son Esau more as he was a talented hunter. Esau, was the firstborn and should have had the right to the blessing of the firstborn; however, this was usurped from him. Jacob was very manipulative in cooking up a pot of lentils (Genesis 25:33-34) and thereby buying the birthright from Esau who was starving following a long hunting trip. Esau's hunger was so intense he was willing to sell the right of the firstborn to his brother Jacob for a pot of soup. Later on in the account, we find Rebecca devising an ingenious plan for Jacob to commit identity fraud by masquerading as his brother Esau. Rebecca knew Isaac had sent Esau out on a hunting trip, as Isaac had a taste for game, and would subsequently bestow the once in a lifetime birthright blessing upon his son following the successful hunting trip. In Esau's absence, Jacob was sent in to Isaac, also with a meal cooked by Rebecca. As Isaac's eyes were weak, he was unable to distinguish the difference between his two sons as Jacob dressed in Esau's clothes that smelt like his brother. The identity trick was complete and Jacob managed to steal the birth right blessing from Esau, after his father ate a goat that was prepared by his wife Rebecca, instead of the wild game. Then we have the shock and trembling disappointment of his Father as the real Esau arrives, which in turn ousts Jacob from his home, followed by murderous threats from his brother. This was a big deal, as the birthright blessing could be given only once. He escapes to Rebecca's family and it is on route to Rebecca's brother Laban that he makes the vow concerning the **tithe**. He is alone, frightened and is facing an uncertain future. He is therefore turning to the only person whom he knows can come to his aid, the God of his ancestors.

²⁰ And Jacob vowed a vow, saying, If God will be with me, and will keep me in this way that I go, and will give me bread to eat, and raiment to put on,

²¹ So that I come again to my father's house in peace; then shall the LORD be my God:

*²² And this stone, which I have set for a pillar, shall be God's house: and of all that thou shalt give me I will surely give **the tenth** unto thee.* **(Genesis 28:2–22) KJV**

In this instance Jacob's vow is an act of desperation. If we review Jacob's character from the beginning and the way he approaches God in this issue, it immediately becomes apparent that no tithe was given at that time and that Jacob's vow was conditional. If the pre-law tithe had already been established under Abraham and Melchizedek, now would have been a good time to put this into practice. It is however clear that this could not be done, as all he had was a dream of Angels descending up and down a ladder and not a physical meeting with God or pre-incarnate Christ. The Levitical priesthood was still in his loins (Israel) and would only appear hundreds of years later. The only thing he understood in this concept was the idea of presenting spoils or tribute of a tenth, which already existed in pagan society. Jacob is making it clear that **if** God will give him food and clothes and establish him safely back to his Father's household, **then** shall the Lord be his God. This is the vow of a person who is seeking to control the situation, even though he has very little bargaining power. It is also unsurprising there is no evidence in the Bible that he actually fulfilled this vow he made to God, neither is there any evidence to suggest that this was possible without a Levitical priesthood to tithe to. The place of Haran was also a pagan area and later on during the Mosaic Law, tithes could only be given from the supernatural increase of the Holy Land in Israel, not Haran. Attempting to strike a bargain with God in advance and attaching the word 'if', does not form a solid basis for a pre-law tithing tradition.

After long and eventful hard lessons, Jacob had to learn with Rebecca's family, following marriage to two women and outsmarting Laban, it then comes to the point that Jacob again is on the run. This time, however, he is running from his father-in-law Laban back to his own father Isaac. Jacob was later renamed by God 'Israel', after he wrestled God till daybreak (Genesis 32: 22-32). Immediately following this experience, Jacob shows his relief by saying:

30 And Jacob called the name of the place Peniel: for I have seen God face to face, and my life is preserved'. **(Genesis 32: 30)**

There is no question we have a clear indication of a pre-incarnate Christ in this reference. Here is the crux of the discussion relating to a supposed pre-law tithe. The Levitical priesthood is within Israel and is still in Jacob's loins

Furthermore, in the account of Jacob's struggle, when God wrestles Jacob till day break, he asks him his name to ascertain if he has come to terms with his identity after pretending to be someone else. Jacob repeats his true name and shows his tenacious nature by refusing to let God go until God blesses him.

26 And he said, Let me go, for the day breaketh. And he said, I will not let thee go, except thou bless me. **(Genesis 32:26) KJV**

Under a pre-law Christian tithing philosophy, God would have had to ask him about the tithe he hadn't paid in order to be blessed. This more than physical meeting and struggle with God would have been the perfect opportunity, but as established earlier, there is no commandment of the sort set anywhere in the book of Genesis.

Tithing: Reviewing Scripture in Context

The Law

Up until now I have made a lot of reference to the words 'pre-law', 'eternal moral principles' and pre-incarnate Christ. These key words are all in reference to establishing the difference between solid Christian Doctrine and some principles in the Old Testament that seem like a good idea to follow, but are no longer a requirement. From the beginning of the first two chapters on Abraham and Jacob, I have outlined what the modern day Church has tried to pass off as a moral law. This does not need to be followed today and has nothing to do with the Mosaic Law, therefore needn't be applicable. As we have seen however, any eternal moral law in this situation does not have solid foundation in scripture. Requiring a tenth of a New Testament congregation's salary based on this evidence is questionable.

When referring to 'eternal moral principles', we would need to first check out the commandments God actually gave under Moses. We also need to consider that the Torah, or Pentateuch was written by Moses and he would have been clear in creating pre-law commandments had there been any. When referring to the Law, we are considering the 613 Mitzvoth (laws) given to Israel. The Orthodox Jews still follow them today, except tithing, as tithing was brought to an end with the sacrificial system in 70AD after the destruction of the temple. Within Christianity, the moral law only applies to the 10 commandments and pretty well little else. For instance, we are not required to perform circumcision as a sign of the covenant with God, neither are we bound by kosher food eating laws or Sabbath keeping. The list is endless!

In replacement theology, preachers and pastors attempt to put themselves into the position of the Levitical priests, in order to receive the tithe. If this were the case, then ministers would all be required to come from a single tribe such as the tribe of Levi. It is in the book of Numbers, that we see the clear move from people who acted as their own priests as with Abraham, Isaac and Jacob to the ordinances of the Levitical priesthood and Aaron. This book is a 40 year record of the Jewish people from Mount Sinai to Canaan. Numbers 18 specifically gives details according to the requirements of tithing and the Levitical priesthood and also the duty requirement of the priests. This included taking on the iniquity of the nation, thus cleansing Israel of all sin.

18 Then the LORD said to Aaron: "You and your sons and your father's house with you shall bear the [b]iniquity related to the sanctuary, and you and your sons with you shall bear the iniquity associated with your priesthood. **(Numbers 18:1)**

Out of the tribe of Levi only a set amount of Levites were actually priests. Levites had many job descriptions as temple workers and acted as assistants to the priests. They were, however, not allowed to take part in the priestly duties, and breaking these commands would have severe consequences. Direct worship in the temple was not permitted for the Levites and it is clear if we review all of Numbers 18, that it was only the priests (Aaronic) who could offer the sacrifices and could only physically consume the food (tithe) in the sanctuary. None of the temple food could leave the Holy Temple for anyone else, the temple food consisting of sacrificed animals, first fruits of oil, wine and grain consisting of one tenth of the tithe. In other words – one tenth of a tithe of a tenth from the nation of Israel. This meant the priests only received a small percentage of the tithe and were not required to tithe of their portion. The Levites who were the assistants to the priests were allowed to take the rest as their portion home to share with their families (Numbers 18-32). The Levites did not have permission to own land and work it, so their lives and ministry were fully funded by food from the Levitical tithe, given to them from the nation of Israel. The Levites lived in 13 specific priestly cities, but did not have ownership of these dwelling places (Joshua 21).

This leads us onto the book that is filled with every possible law you can think of in relation to Israel. The book of Leviticus.

*'Nevertheless no [10]devoted offering that a man may devote to the LORD of all that he has, both man and beast, or the field of his possession, shall be sold or redeemed; every devoted offering is most holy to the LORD. [29] No person under the ban, who may become doomed to destruction among men, shall be redeemed, but shall surely be put to death. [30] **And all the tithe of the land, whether of the seed of the land or of the fruit of the tree, is the LORD's. It is holy to the LORD.** [31] If a man wants at all to redeem any of his tithes, he shall add one-fifth to it. [32] And concerning the tithe of the herd or the flock, of whatever passes under the rod, the tenth one shall be holy to the LORD. [33] He shall not inquire whether it is good or bad, nor shall he exchange it; and if he exchanges it at all, then both it and the one exchanged for it shall be holy; it shall not be redeemed."*

[34] These are the commandments which the LORD commanded Moses for the children of Israel on Mount Sinai. **(Leviticus 27: 28-34)**

Here the recurring theme is 'Holy to the Lord', or even, 'you shall be holy to Me, for I the Lord am Holy, and have separated you from the peoples, that you should be mine' (Leviticus 20:26). God is preoccupied in this book with teaching the Mosaic Law to the people, whereby holiness is the obedience to the law in every chapter. It is important to understand that the 'Holy' aspect of the law, is to stay in the confines of the Mosaic Law, relevant only to the children of Israel during the time of the Old Covenant. It is true that the tithe was considered to be holy to the Lord, but so were all the other things that were mentioned including, offerings, consecration, atonement, religious festivals, food laws, redemption laws, devoted things, and lastly **'tithing'**. (Kelly 2007 p44). If you choose to resurrect **tithing** from the Levitical statutes, then you would need to resurrect all the other statutes of the law as well. As the Apostle Paul writes:

[10] *For as many as are of the works of the law are under the curse; for it is written, "Cursed is everyone who does not continue in **all** things which are written in the book of the law, to do them."* [11] *But that no one is [a]justified by the law in the sight of God is evident, for "the just shall live by faith."* **(Galatians 3:10-11)**

'The just shall live by faith', is evidently the New Covenant requirement. Clearly none of the former Levitical principles have been adopted by the New Testament Church as still 'Holy to the Lord', so why is the same method or request applied to the tithe as an eternal moral principle? The Laws and statutes were laid down by God to support a theocracy and to meet the needs of every person of Israel in a system which was also meant to cover the poor and the needy. It was an ancient system of Welfare Government. The context pertaining to the audience of Leviticus is further reinforced by verse 34 namely: 'The Children of Israel'!

The Mosaic Law is given to Moses during the 40 years in the wilderness; however, this was not the case for the tithe. One might ask, if the law was given, why was it not put into operation? The Children of Israel literally had to do nothing during this time and Manna fell from heaven during that time period, up until the very time they crossed over into what was to be the promised Land of Israel. No one had been given land to plant as an inheritance in the desert, or owned land. The very reason the Levites were to receive the tithe, was for the very reason that they were not given land. Furthermore, tithes could only be given from the supernatural increase of the Holy Land. Tithes from any other pagan soil was not considered Holy to the Lord. One is therefore not able to evidentially justify any type of tithing, unless it is directly linked to the Holy Land.

As we are commenting on when tithing was not to take place, it is therefore necessary to talk about the 7th and 50th year in the Holy Land. Tithes could only be produced and distributed in Israel, furthermore for the purpose of crop rotation and the need for the land to rest, no tithe was paid on the 7th year, when the poor and needy could also glean from the fields. The 50th year marked the Jubilee year and was also marked as a time when the tithe was not to take place, but the food had to be taken straight from the field. (Kelly 2007 p 59)

11 but the seventh year you shall let it rest and lie fallow, that the poor of your people may eat; and what they leave, the beasts of the field may eat. In like manner you shall do with your vineyard and your [a]olive grove. **Exodus 23:11**

12 For it is the Jubilee; it shall be holy to you; you shall eat its produce from the field.

13 'In this Year of Jubilee, each of you shall return to his possession. **Leviticus 25:12-13**

Can you imagine if a congregation would return to their pastor for a tax rebate on behalf of having paid tithes on the 7th year or even 50th Jubilee year for a very long standing member? As mentioned earlier, you can't follow some aspects of the law. You have to follow them all! If tithing is a statute a person chooses to follow, then one needs to follow the exact rules and regulations they are governed by. This includes the types of tithes that were given. Were there different types of tithes you ask? That leads us on nicely to the next chapter.

Tithing: Reviewing Scripture in Context

Bring your Tithe(s) to the store house?

As already discovered and defined, the tithe meant 10% of crop, herd, oil or wine. It was a food source that was in supply to the Levites as they were unable to own land and was therefore their portion. It could only be sourced from the Holy Land of Israel and no other pagan land. Have you ever wondered why the word tithes is often written in plural? Is it because a person pays their 'tithe' and the congregation 'tithes', in other words plural because there are more than one person taking part? This is the aspect to the subject that surprises a lot of people, as we lack detail when reading scripture especially when Leviticus, Numbers and Deuteronomy are concerned. We are far less concerned with the aspects of the law which we know do not apply to us, but would rather inform ourselves from the historical books in the Bible. There is, however, a reason why tithe(s) is written in plural, as there were not just one of them, which also leads on to a very important question. If you are invoking the tithe as an eternal moral principle to be made applicable to the modern day Church, which tithe is it you are asking for or paying? There are three to choose from:

1. The Levitical tithe to be collected once a year.
2. The Festival tithe to be collected once a year.
3. The Poor tithe that was to be collected every three years.

The existence of three tithes can be confirmed by Flavius Josephus, a Jewish historian from whom we glean a lot of historical reference during this time period. Josephus is often quoted to verify the historical accuracy of the Bible.

"In addition to the two tithes which I have already directed you to pay each year, the one for the Levites and the other for the banquets, ye should devote a third every third year to the distribution

of such things as are lacking to widowed women and orphan children."–Antiquities iv. 240; Loeb ed.

The first tithe (Levitical) we have covered in length as it was the Levitical tithe. If ministers are collecting what they believe to be the Levitical tithe, then they clearly are not allowed to own land. The Levites were all from the tribe of Levi some of which were Aaronic priests. The 10% would go to the Levites and 10% of this tithe would go to the priests. The priestly tithe had to stay in the store house and be eaten in the Temple area, whereas the rest of the tithe for the Levites could be carried off the temple site and be taken home to their families, or to one of the 13 Levitical cities. And again, it could only come from the Holy Land of Israel.

[20] Then the LORD said to Aaron: "You shall have no inheritance in their land, nor shall you have any portion among them; I am your portion and your inheritance among the children of Israel.

[21] "Behold, I have given the children of Levi all the tithes in Israel as [a]an inheritance in return for the work which they perform, the work of the tabernacle of meeting. (**Numbers 18:20-21**)

The second tithe (Festival) was the tithe that was brought directly to Jerusalem the Holy City. The Israelites who had produce from their land, orchards, vineyards and herds would take this tithe to Jerusalem once a year and it was almost in the form of a family holiday. This tithe was in support of the festivals and a portion was consumed with the Levites in celebration with the tither's entire family. It formed a time of festivity and celebration in the presence of the Lord.

[6] There you shall take your burnt offerings, your sacrifices, your tithes, the heave offerings of your hand, your vowed

offerings, your freewill offerings, and the firstborn of your herds and flocks. [7] And there you shall eat before the LORD your God, and you shall rejoice in [a] all to which you have put your hand, you and your households, in which the LORD your God has blessed you. **(Deuteronomy 12:6-7)**

If you choose to go with the argument that they simply tithed food, as there was no financial system, then the following scripture will let you know that **money** was readily available and used as a form of exchange, not just a bartering system. The only time it was acceptable to use money was for the festival tithe, and only if the meeting place was too far to travel, as food could spoil. It was a logistical issue.

*[24] But if the journey is too long for you, so that you are not able to carry the **tithe**, or if the place where the LORD your God chooses to put His name is too far from you, when the LORD your God has blessed you, [25] then you shall exchange it for money, take the money in your hand, and go to the place which the LORD your God chooses. [26] And you shall spend that money for whatever your heart desires: for oxen or sheep, for wine or similar drink, for whatever your heart desires; you shall eat there before the LORD your God, and you shall rejoice, you and your household. [27] You shall not [a] forsake the Levite who is within your gates, for he has no part nor inheritance with you'.* **Deuteronomy 14:24-27**

The third tithe (Tri annual poor tithe) was for whom the name actually suggests. It took place every 3 years. It wasn't just for the widow and the orphan; it was also for the stranger who was not originally from Israel. (Side note, strangers to Israel were not allowed to tithe; more on this later!) This tithe went to the place it was needed in Israel and not specifically the Holy city. We have therefore, three distinctly different tithes.

[28] "At the end of every third year you shall bring out the tithe of your produce of that year and store it up within your gates.

[29] And the Levite, because he has no portion nor inheritance with you, and the stranger and the fatherless and the widow who are within your gates, may come and eat and be satisfied, that the LORD your God may bless you in all the work of your hand which you do. **(Deuteronomy 14:28-29)**

[12] "When you have finished laying aside all the tithe of your increase in the third year—the year of tithing—and have given it to the Levite, the stranger, the fatherless, and the widow, so that they may eat within your gates and be filled, [13] then you shall say before the LORD your God: 'I have removed the [a]holy tithe from my house, and also have given them to the Levite, the stranger, the fatherless, and the widow, according to all Your commandments which You have commanded me; I have not transgressed Your commandments, nor have I forgotten them'. **(Deuteronomy 26:12-13)**

Bringing the whole tithes (plural) into the storehouse, is clearly because there were three of them. Not just more than one person tithing. This also causes a discrepancy with the expectation to tithe merely 10%. The tithe consisted of 10% Levitical tithe, 10% Festival tithe and lastly the tri-annual poor tithe consisting of 3.3% every year. This was a yearly combined tithe of **23.3%**. I have yet to experience any pastor preaching a sermon on this, furthermore requiring the congregation to tithe this amount. If you believe in literal replacement theology, in other words the Church replacing the Jewish people with their ordinances and statutes, then this is the percentage to be required. Three tithes of which 2 are 10% a year and 1 every 3 years, culminating in 23.3% of income. Then tithing on every 7th year and 50th Jubilee year would also need to cease.

44

Taxation or Tithing?

Taxation has never been a popular thing, especially when going to church requires it. Ironically it was Adolf Hitler who introduced a Church tax in 1939 in Germany, which was even retained after the Second World War and was based on the system of the tithe. In Germany the church tax is currently very controversial and is keeping the churches empty. Up to 400 000 people in 2015 have filed declaration to leave the Catholic and Protestant church after the decision was made to extend an 8 to 9% to Capital Gains income. People have continued to leave the churches in Germany in droves ever since. Germans have been trying to hide their true salary figures, in order to prevent this from taking place. These thousands of Germans are writing written declarations formally renouncing their faith, in order to escape the not so 'free will giving'. This tax is there to fund all church activities and is collected by the state. Qualification for this tax is dependent on Baptism. If the tax is not paid, then people may be prevented from attending church schools or relinquish their rights to a Christian burial. For Catholics this is especially damaging, as the faith is directly linked to the receiving of the sacraments, of which confession and communion are the most important *(Justin Huggler 2015)*.

You may wonder why I have mentioned this dilemma in Germany, but it serves to inform us of the danger of enforcing financial systems on the body of Christ as a whole, especially when it is not evidential in scripture. When the love of God is removed from the privilege of giving, you are just left with an atmosphere of contempt. The interference of the state in the tithing system was, however, not a completely new thing. Tithing started in the Land of Israel when the children of Israel had finally inherited this Promised Land, but over the hundreds of years of Israel's history, there were many instances when tithing either came to a complete stop due to running after other Gods, or if the ruling Jewish monarch had turned their hearts to paganism, or even if Israel was an occupied nation and the first tithe may have gone to the ruling empire. The book of Judges is characterised by the very notion that each man had come to the point that they were making up their own rules for living and therefore, not following the statutes of God. This temporarily put a hold on strict ritualised tithing and the Levitical priesthood was in disarray.

[25] In those days there was no king in Israel; everyone did what was right in his own eyes'. **Judges 21:25**

A King is what the people wanted and a King is what they received and we see the prophet Samuel who was the last Judge anoint such a person as their leader and spiritual head. The ruling monarch then became the person to receive the all-important 1st tithe, which cannot be described as anything less than a tax.

[10] So Samuel told all the words of the LORD to the people who asked him for a king. [11] And he said, "This will be the behaviour of the king who will reign over you: He will take your sons and appoint them for his own chariots and to be his horsemen, and some will run before his chariots. [12] He will appoint captains over his thousands and captains over his fifties, will set some to plough his ground and reap his harvest, and some to make his weapons of war and equipment for his chariots. [13] He will take your daughters to be perfumers, cooks, and bakers. [14] And he will take the best of your fields, your vineyards, and your olive groves, and give them to his servants. [15] He will take a tenth of your grain and your vintage, and give it to his officers and servants. [16] And he will take your male servants, your female servants, your finest [a] young men, and your donkeys, and put them to his work. [17] He will take a tenth of your sheep. And you will be his servants'. **Samuel 8:10-17**

Following the disastrous years of King Saul we find a new King emerge, more in line with God's heart, who used the Levites not just as Religious workers, but gave them governmental responsibilities (1Chron. 23:2-4; 1Chron 26:29-32). This meant that King David and his successor Solomon had Kingship and control over the Levites including the tithes they were collecting. This would have looked commonplace in the surrounding cultures where the monarch was the highest authority and therefore, equivalent to the more modern day defender of the faith. This is the type of model used on behalf of governments that integrated Church and State, whereby you would have a mixture of civil and religious taxation. So what points do we glean from these pieces of evidence?

It is clear to see that the restructuring by King David and Solomon indicates the Levites were not full time in ministry. They would have had religious duties mixed with governmental responsibilities, indicating that just a fraction of their time was assigned to temple duties. How the New Covenant Church can insist on a tithe from congregants based on these Old Testament systems of taxation and call it evidential according to scripture, preys upon those who are too intimidated to pick up a Bible and read it for themselves. Even the priests received only 10% of the 10% tithe. 9% of the tithe therefore went to the Levites who did not own land. Do all churches nowadays that accept the tithing system have lots of church workers running around full time with the Pastor collecting 1% for himself? Basing a doctrine on a Welfare system also based on taxation is for the most part peculiar. The modern day Christian will believe most things if it relates to the teachings of the Church, as the elders and ministers for the most part do not know these things and are likely to keep quiet about it if they do. How much better would it be if the leaders indeed would pick up a Bible and check out the evidences for themselves?

A very important point to address in relation to the title of this chapter is regarding the Welfare State. Israel had a Welfare system within the tithes. If you are living in a country that runs a generous benefit system, which is typical for all western countries today, then it is likely that you are paying a substantial amount of money to the State for the upkeep of council housing and other financial needs. This is generally removed from your pay cheque before you receive it. Therefore, if you are a person who is employed, you are already supporting the poor through the tax system set up by the Welfare system. This is what the Old Testament tithe was for!

Foodbanks: A Present Day Tithe?

As we established at the beginning of this book, tithing was either due to spoils of war/tribute or in the sense of the Mosaic Law was theocratic and only included **food** and went only to the Levites for distribution. The Zondervan Bible Dictionary defined the latter as the following.

*Mosaic law required tithing of all **produce of land and herds** (Lev, 27:30-33); use for support of Levites and priests (Num. 18. 21-32); additional tithes may have been required at certain times (Deut. 12:5-18; 14:22-29); there were penalties for cheating in tithing (Lev. 27:31; Deut. 26; 13-15). Pharisees tithed even **herbs** Matt. 22:23; Luke 11:42).* **(Zondervan Bible Dictionary)**

In repetition to what has already be presented and with the emphasis of bold type, the scriptures to support this were:

*[30] And all the tithe of the land, whether of the **seed of the land or of the fruit of the tree**, is the LORD's. It is holy to the LORD. [31] If a man wants at all to redeem any of his tithes, he shall add one-fifth to it. [32] And concerning the tithe of the **herd or the flock**, of whatever passes under the rod, the tenth one shall be holy to the LORD. [33] He shall not inquire whether it is good or bad, nor shall he exchange it; and if he exchanges it at all, then both it and the one exchanged for it shall be holy; it shall not be redeemed.'* **Leviticus 27:30-33**

*[21] "Behold, I have given the children of Levi all the **tithes** in Israel as an inheritance in return for the work which they perform, the work of the tabernacle of meeting. [22] Hereafter the children of Israel shall not come near the tabernacle of meeting, lest they bear sin and die. [23] But the Levites shall perform the work of the tabernacle of meeting, and they shall bear their iniquity; it shall be a statute forever, throughout*

*your generations, that among the children of Israel they shall
have no inheritance'.* **Numbers 18:21-23**

[5] *"But you shall seek the place where the LORD your God
chooses, out of all your tribes, to put His name for His
dwelling[c] place; and there you shall go. [6] There you shall take
your burnt offerings, your sacrifices, your* **tithes**, *the heave
offerings of your hand, your vowed offerings, your freewill
offerings, and the firstborn of your* **herds** *and* **flocks**. *[7] And
there you shall* **eat** *before the LORD your God, and you shall
rejoice in [d] all to which you have put your hand, you and your
households, in which the LORD your God has blessed you.*

[8] *"You shall not at all do as we are doing here today—every
man doing whatever is right in his own eyes— [9] for as yet you
have not come to the rest and the inheritance which the
LORD your God is giving you. [10] But when you cross over the
Jordan and dwell in the land which the LORD your God is
giving you to inherit, and He gives you rest from all your
enemies round about, so that you dwell in safety, [11] then there
will be the place where the LORD your God chooses to make
His name abide. There you shall bring all that I command
you: your burnt offerings, your sacrifices, your* **tithes**, *the
heave offerings of your hand, and all your choice offerings
which you vow to the LORD. [12] And you shall rejoice before
the LORD your God, you and your sons and your daughters,
your male and female servants, and the Levite who is within
your gates, since he has no portion nor inheritance with you.
[13] Take heed to yourself that you do not offer your burnt
offerings in every place that you see; [14] but in the place which
the LORD chooses, in one of your tribes, there you shall offer
your burnt offerings, and there you shall do all that I
command you.*

[15] *"However, you may slaughter and* **eat** *meat within all your
gates, whatever your heart desires, according to the blessing of*

the LORD *your God which He has given you; the unclean and the clean may eat of it, of the gazelle and the deer alike.* [16] *Only you shall not* **eat** *the blood; you shall pour it on the earth like water.* [17] **You may not eat within your gates the tithe of your grain or your new wine or your oil, of the firstborn of your herd or your flock, of any of your offerings which you vow, of your freewill offerings, or of the** [t]**heave offering of your hand.** [18] *But you must* **eat** *them before the* LORD *your God in the place which the* LORD *your God chooses, you and your son and your daughter, your male servant and your female servant, and the Levite who is within your gates; and you shall rejoice before the* LORD *your God in* [u]*all to which you put your hands'.* **Deuteronomy 12:5-18**

As a reminder, the only relation of 'money' to the word 'tithe' in scripture, is when the place of meeting was too far to travel. It therefore, could be sold with the use of money in order to once again buy it back in the form of 'food and drink' to be physically consumed. The tithe, I repeat, could only be given in the form of 'food and drink', with the Levites and the family rejoicing before the Lord. This is the only evidence of scripture linking the tithe to money, but it was converted back to food.

[22] *"You shall truly* **tithe all the increase of your grain that the field produces year by year.** [23] *And you shall* **eat** *before the* LORD *your God, in the place where He chooses to make His name abide, the* **tithe** *of your grain and your new wine and your oil, of the firstborn of your herds and your flocks, that you may learn to fear the* LORD *your God always.* [24] *But if the journey is too long for you, so that you are not able to carry the tithe, or if the place where the* LORD *your God chooses to put His name is too far from you, when the* LORD *your God has blessed you,* [25] *then you shall* **exchange it for money,** *take the money in your hand, and go to the place which the* LORD *your God chooses.* [26] *And you shall spend that money*

for whatever your heart desires: for oxen or sheep, for wine or similar drink, for whatever your heart desires; **you shall eat there before the LORD your God, and you shall rejoice, you and your household.** *[a]You shall not [a]forsake the Levite who is within your gates, for he has no part nor inheritance with you.*

[28]"At the end of every third year you shall bring out the tithe of your produce of that year and store it up within your gates. [29]And the Levite, because he has no portion nor inheritance with you, and the stranger and the fatherless and the widow who are within your gates, may come and **eat and be satisfied,** *that the LORD your God may bless you in all the work of your hand which you do'.* **Deuteronomy 14:22-29**

With this evidence set in place, that the tithe was only ever in relation to food, I would now like to draw a modern day need and comparison with the above verses Deuteronomy 14: 28-29. Although the modern day church is not required to tithe according to established Christian Doctrine, there are those who still will maintain that it is either an eternal moral principle starting with Abraham and Jacob, required by the Mosaic law that we should be following, or even a mixture of the two required today. I covered tithe or taxation in the previous chapter with links to the modern day, so I will draw a modern day comparison for those who still want to remain steadfast with the principle of tithing. I will first need to ask questions. Are you paying the tithe as a form of tribute/spoils of war/taxation due to a pre-law principle in line with Abraham and Jacob who **did not tithe out of their own goods?** This question you may have already asked yourself, and answered, when entering the evidence of the possibility of viewing Melchizedek as a pre-incarnate Christ. The other question I need to ask, is concerning the tithe that you are deciding to pay in respect of money. There are many instances of currency used as exchange in Genesis alone, and copious references in the entire Old Testament:

"And Abram was very rich in cattle, in silver, and in gold". **Genesis 13:2**

"So it was, when the camels had finished drinking, that the man took a golden nose ring weighing half a shekel, and two bracelets for her wrists weighing ten shekels of gold". **Genesis 24:22**

It can therefore be established, that although systems of currency were used even during the time of Genesis and throughout the Old Testament, food is the only source of giving for the Tithe! Therefore, if you really feel convicted to obey this Old Testament principle in accordance with replacement theology, then you would be required to replace like for like and indeed pay your tithe to the Church in the form of food and drink! I can see a raised eyebrow or two if you were to try and do this when the offering plate is passed around. Furthermore, attempting to follow the 23.3% tithe requirement of 3 tithes, two of which annually and one of which every 3 years. May I also suggest in most cases you would require large transportation to do so?

From a theocratic perspective, it is clear why God required the tithe in the form of food only for the Levites, who kept a portion for themselves and organised a portion also for the poor in respect of the orphan, widow and the stranger. (Deuteronomy 14:18-19) The system was safe, as people were thus unable to use the goods for anything else than physical consumption and was indeed the Judaic form of welfare and in some instances taxation.

I would like to mention some statistics regarding the poor in my home country. In a modern day setting the welfare system in the UK is so broken down, that *food bank usage* in 2018 has reached its highest rate on record as the benefit system has failed to cover basic costs. At the time of writing the UK population has reached 66,865,998. This figure is of course changing daily due to births and deaths, but still with an upward trend. The urban population consists of about 80% of the population with an astonishing 1,332,952 requiring three-day emergency food supplies delivered. This is a 13 % increase on 2017, with a 6% increase the year before. Referral to foodbanks comes as a result, not just due to people on benefits, but also to those who are in the bracket of low income. The problem with inflation is directly linked to the need for foodbanks, as benefits and salaries are often not uprated in line with inflation, rising food costs and general cost of living. People as a result are turning to food banks in order to eat. Surprisingly 1 out of 6 people requiring assistance from food banks are working. These statistics are being collected during a time when the UK has a record 3.2 million more people in work since 2010. (**May Bulman**, Social affairs Correspondent, 'Food bank use in UK reaches highest rate on record as benefits fail to cover basic costs', Independent 24 April 2018) Now you may be wondering why I am making this link and drawing on these statistics? The answer is evidently simple. If you want to honour the idea of a Biblical context to tithing, Foodbanks would indeed be your perfect opportunity!

The unfortunate truth is, anyone actually requiring assistance of the church among the congregation in many cases, will have had pressure put on them to tithe, despite their financial position and being unable to provide for their basic needs or family. The old slogan of 'God being able to help you more if you tithe the 10% and only keeping the 90%', becomes a little tiresome, when even the middleclass families with both parents working may struggle to do so. After a while this philosophy becomes nothing more than actually the Pharisees devouring widows' houses:

⁴⁷ who devour widows' houses, and for a pretence make long prayers. These will receive greater condemnation." **Luke 20:47**

If we consider the amount some Pastors and TV evangelists earn with the philosophy of the tithe and the giving of offerings, it does indeed put the above verse in a modern day context. This kind of thing does become increasingly likely when you have widows who have no one else than their TV screens to keep them company and viewing prosperity preachers becomes their only form of company, or even involvement in a community.

The behaviour of the people in charge in the temple was often a source of annoyance for God, as the Priests did not always do as they were told. Eli the High priest and his sons were punished during the time of the Judges, due to bad leadership (Samuel 4), leading to the glory departing. This in the Old Testament, however, was not an unusual occurrence. The Priests in the last book of the Bible, Malachi, also behaved badly in regard to lazy worship and theft, which leads us on to the next chapter.

Tithing: Reviewing Scripture in Context

Malachi: Dissecting the book in context

The book of Malachi is the last prophetic book in the Old Testament. The Jews were waiting for their Messiah and Malachi is the last prophet before John the Baptist. Malachi does indeed prepare a way, as it is a book of correction addressing particularly the priests in a post-exilic Judah. But who was Malachi? He was one of the three prophets amongst Zechariah and Haggai. The time is set during Ezra the scribe and much context to the book is given to us by Nehemiah. What we can ascertain from the Hebrew, is that his name means 'messenger'. If we look at Judaic sources, there are some that suggest he was indeed Ezra the scribe, although others may suggest he may have been Mordecai from the book of Esther. Most Talmudic Jews, however, maintain that he was not any of these, but his own person (Talmud, Megillah 15a). This position is also taken from most Biblical historians today. We do however know, that he was part of the great Assembly that met in Jerusalem during the initial stages of the second temple era, which Judaic sources also agree with (Talmud, Bava Batra 15a and Megillah 17B).

Malachi is quite a short book and easy to read, yet most people are only familiar with the verses about tithing. The structure of the book is outlined as the following:

Malachi 2:1-9; Malachi criticizes the leaders for not teaching the Law.

Malachi 2:10-16; Malachi addresses the unequal yoking of intermarriage with other tribes whilst   divorcing their own wives.

Malachi 3:6-12; Malachi expresses God's distaste for the way the priests are trying to rob God by stealing the tithes.

If you are well versed in the tithing philosophy of the modern day Church, then Malachi 3:8-11 will not have escaped your attention. It is chiefly the only scripture most congregants are aware of concerning tithing, as it promises untold blessing if followed and the release of the devourer if disobeyed.

> *"Will a man rob God?*
> *Yet you have robbed Me!*
> *But you say,*
> *'In what way have we robbed You?'*
> *In tithes and offerings.*
> *⁹ You are cursed with a curse,*
> *For you have robbed Me,*
> *Even this whole nation.*
> *¹⁰ Bring all the tithes into the storehouse,*
> *That there may be **food** in My house,*
> *And try Me now in this,"*
> *Says the LORD of hosts,*
> *"If I will not open for you the windows of heaven*
> *And pour out for you such blessing*
> *That there will not be room enough to receive it.*
>
> *¹¹ "And I will rebuke the devourer for your sakes,*
> *So that he will not destroy the fruit of your ground,*
> *Nor shall the vine fail to bear fruit for you in the field,"*
> *Says the LORD of hosts '.* **Malachi 3: 8 -11**

Unfortunately, no context of the book of Malachi is usually ever given by tithe teaching churches. No historical books are mentioned either to gain an insight as to why Malachi is prophesying these things, let alone any other topics within Malachi. I would go as far to say, that these verses are the most misused in the Bible, giving people over to exploitation due to lack of knowledge. Only very few people even know that tithes were given in **food**. Even the favourite verses above confirm that it was food. The gaps of knowledge relating to

Malachi are not always just on behalf of the congregation, but largely by the Ministers as well, who are merely regurgitating what they have previously been taught. People in this respect are not encouraged to read the Bible in detail or context. These verses are firmly ingrained into the psyche of the modern-day believer and are used as a minimum standard of giving, with the supposed giving of the tithe opening the windows of heaven, and the offerings as seed of increase. This principle comes with the promise of 'pie in the sky', and justification for the release of finances into the life of the modern day believer. Kingdom principles, we are given to believe, were set down by Jesus as eternal moral principles.

As mentioned earlier, it is the context of these verses which is so very important. The context to the prophetic book of Malachi are likely to be in the historical accounts given to us by Nehemiah. We are informed that the audience this book is addressed to, are the 'Israelites', who are under the Law and under an oath to ensure God's law is kept; furthermore, under a curse if the Law is broken. The audience for these verses are not for a New Testament church congregation.

28' And the rest of the people, the priests, the Levites, the porters, the singers, the Nethinims, and all they that had separated themselves from the people of the lands unto the law of God, their wives, their sons, and their daughters, every one having knowledge, and having understanding;

29 They clave to their brethren, their nobles, and entered into a **curse,** *and into an oath, to walk in God's law, which was given by Moses the servant of God, and to observe and do all the commandments of the LORD our Lord, and his judgments and his statutes'.* **Nehemiah 10:28-29**

They were instructed to bring the tithes and first fruits (single bushels of wheat, grain or fruit from the tree small enough to carry in a basket) into the storehouse. First fruits or the 'offering', were given by the children of Israel. The storehouse as we discovered earlier in this book was in relation to the Levitical tithe (or referred to as 'Children of Levi), 10% of which went to the Levites and 10% of that amount to the priests (1%), to be held in the temple chambers storehouse, whereas the Levitical portion could be taken and consumed in the Levitical cities away from the temple area.

*"³⁴ We, the priests, the Levites, and the people, have likewise cast lots for the wood offering, to bring it into the house of our God, according to our fathers' houses, at times appointed, year by year, to burn on the altar of the LORD our God, as it is written in the Law. ³⁵ We obligate ourselves to bring the firstfruits of our ground and the firstfruits of all fruit of every tree, year by year, to the house of the LORD; ³⁶ also to bring to the house of our God, to the priests who minister in the house of our God, the firstborn of our sons and of our cattle, as it is written in the Law, and the firstborn of our herds and of our flocks; ³⁷ and to bring the first of our dough, and our contributions, the fruit of every tree, the wine and the oil, to the priests, to the chambers of the house of our God; and to bring to the Levites the **tithes** from our ground, for it is the Levites who collect the **tithes** in all our towns where we labour. ³⁸ And the priest, the son of Aaron, shall be with the Levites when the Levites receive the **tithes**. And the Levites shall bring up the tithe of the tithes to the house of our God, to the chambers of the storehouse'.* **Nehemiah 10-34-38**

The specific context to the most famous verses in Malachi about robbing God comes into play, when we realise how the priests were behaving. This is likely to be the true and actual context of the verses in relation to robbing God. The priests who were entitled to 10% of the 10% were neglecting the Levites and robbing them of their portion. As a result, the temple had to be shut down, as the Levites decided to go to the fields to work them in order to feed themselves, neglecting their part time temple shifts. The High priest Eliashib and

Tobiah the Ammonite (related to Eliashib by marriage) were certainly not living their lives in favour of Israel. Tobiah was in direct opposition to Nehemiah's restoration and rebuilding of the walls of Jerusalem and gained favour with Eliashib the High Priest, who leased the store rooms of the Temple to him, thus allowing him to flourish bountifully in business. These store rooms were of course for the tithes. Nehemiah gained permission from Artaxerxes of Persia to return to the newly constructed temple in Jerusalem and restore the correct order, furthermore returning the storehouse to its proper and holy use. This required the necessary ritualised cleansing to allow this to take place, and the ejecting of Tobiah the Ammonite from the area. This is explained in Nehemiah 13:4-12:

'And before this, Eliashib the priest, having the oversight of the chamber of the house of our God, was allied unto Tobiah:

⁵ And he had prepared for him a great chamber, where aforetime they laid the meat offerings, the frankincense, and the vessels, and the tithes of the corn, the new wine, and the oil, which was commanded to be given to the Levites, and the singers, and the porters; and the offerings of the priests.

⁶ But in all this time was not I at Jerusalem: for in the two and thirtieth year of Artaxerxes king of Babylon came I unto the king, and after certain days obtained I leave of the king:

⁷ And I came to Jerusalem, and understood of the evil that Eliashib did for Tobiah, in preparing him a chamber in the courts of the house of God.

⁸ And it grieved me sore: therefore I cast forth all the household stuff to Tobiah out of the chamber.

⁹ Then I commanded, and they cleansed the chambers: and

thither brought I again the vessels of the house of God, with the meat offering and the frankincense.

[10] And I perceived that the portions of the Levites had not been given them: for the Levites and the singers, that did the work, were fled everyone to his field.

[11] Then contended I with the rulers, and said, Why is the house of God forsaken? And I gathered them together, and set them in their place.

[12] Then brought all Judah the tithe of the corn and the new wine and the oil unto the treasuries'. **Nehemiah 13:4-12**

Now with this knowledge we can apply the context to what God is communicating in Malachi 3:8-1. The Priests were indeed robbing God of tithes and offerings and stealing the portion that was due the Levites. This verse is not for a New Testament church leadership to use to convince a congregation into paying tithes, promising untold open-heaven riches if they obey, and a curse if they do not. The whole irony of the situation is, it is a rebuke of the very leadership who were selfishly withholding food from the poor. Already in Malachi chapter 1, leading into chapter 2, God is setting the record straight concerning his feelings relating to the behaviour of the priests:

> *"A son honours his father,*
> *And a servant his master.*
> *If then I am the Father,*
> *Where is My honour?*
> *And if I am a Master,*
> *Where is My reverence?*
> *Says the LORD of hosts*
> *To you priests who despise My name.*
> *Yet you say, 'In what way have we despised Your*

name?'

⁷ *"You offer defiled food on My altar,*
But say,
'In what way have we defiled You?'
By saying,
'The table of the LORD is [a]*contemptible.'*
⁸ *And when you offer the blind as a sacrifice,*
Is it not evil?
And when you offer the lame and sick,
Is it not evil?
Offer it then to your governor!
Would he be pleased with you?
Would he accept [b] *you favourably?"*
Says the LORD of hosts.

⁹ *"But now entreat God's favour,*
That He may be gracious to us.
While this is being done by your hands,
Will He accept you favourably?"
Says the LORD of hosts.
¹⁰ *"Who is there even among you who would shut the*
doors,
So that you would not kindle fire on My altar in
vain?
I have no pleasure in you,"
Says the LORD of hosts,
"Nor will I accept an offering from your hands.
¹¹ *For from the rising of the sun, even to its going*
down,
My name shall be great among the Gentiles;
In every place incense shall be offered to My name,
And a pure offering;
For My name shall be great among the nations,"
Says the LORD of hosts.

[12] *"But you profane it,*
In that you say,
'The table of the [c] *LORD is defiled;*
And its fruit, its food, is contemptible.'
[13] *You also say,*
'Oh, what a weariness!'
And you sneer at it,"
Says the LORD of hosts.
"And you bring the stolen, the lame, and the sick;
Thus you bring an offering!
Should I accept this from your hand?"
Says the LORD.
[14] *"But cursed be the deceiver*
Who has in his flock a male,
And takes a vow,
But sacrifices to the Lord what is blemished—
For I am a great King,"
Says the LORD of hosts,
"And My name is to be feared among the nations.

2 "And now, O priests, this commandment is for
you.
[2] *If you will not hear,*
And if you will not take it to heart,
To give glory to My name,"
Says the LORD of hosts,
"I will send a curse upon you,
And I will curse your blessings.
Yes, I have cursed them already,
Because you do not take it to heart.

[3] *"Behold, I will rebuke your descendants*
And spread refuse on your faces,
The refuse of your solemn feasts;
And one will take you away [d] *with it.*
[4] *Then you shall know that I have sent this*

commandment to you,
That My covenant with Levi may continue,"
Says the LORD of hosts.
⁵ "My covenant was with him, one of life and peace,
And I gave them to him that he might fear Me;
So he feared Me
And was reverent before My name.
⁶ The⁽ᵃ⁾ law of truth was in his mouth,
And ⁽ᵇ⁾injustice was not found on his lips.
He walked with Me in peace and equity,
And turned many away from iniquity.

⁷ "For the lips of a priest should keep knowledge,
And people should seek the law from his mouth;
For he is the messenger of the LORD of hosts.
⁸ But you have departed from the way;
You have caused many to stumble at the law.
You have corrupted the covenant of Levi,"
Says the LORD of hosts.
⁹ "Therefore I also have made you contemptible and
base
Before all the people,
Because you have not kept My ways
But have shown partiality in the law."

Malachi 1:6 – 2:9

God is rebuking in a question asking and answering like style, usually used by teachers scolding children. I will paraphrase the above into the general gist for emphasis: *Where is my honour? Where is my reverence? To you* **priests** *who despise my name? Yet you say, in what way have we despised your name? Offering blind diseased animals on my altar – try serving them up to your boss, is he going to accept you? Would he give you favour in return? Stop lighting useless fires on my altar! A matter of fact, you might as well shut up shop and lock the temple doors! And you complain saying: 'what* *a burden' (weariness)! And you just stick your nose up! You are not offering me the best you have vowed, but are giving me the worst! Therefore, I will curse your blessing. Effectively, I have cursed them already!*

This all sets the scene in the build-up, for when God rebukes the priests, as they are committing theft and robbing God also in tithes and offerings in Malachi 3:8-11. When reading the whole of Malachi in context to whom the book is addressed (Israelites), and the people who were actually being rebuked (the priests), it is very hard to envisage any common sense in regard to using these verses to support a tithe paying church. When dissecting the book of Malachi, God is rebuking the priests for not obeying the law, leaving their wives for foreign women and lastly for stealing the Levitical portion of the tithe. This account of the sin of the priests relating to leaving their Jewish wives for foreign women is also supported in Nehemiah (Neh. 13:23-30) (2:14-16). Interestingly enough, you will have far more said about the topic of tithing in Nehemiah compared with Malachi. There is much to be said for reading the whole book of Malachi, which only has 4 short chapters, especially if you are considering paying 10% of your hard earned income to obey the law. Even if we ignore the system of paying 3 tithes, it does seriously put into question the percentage of the tithe in modern day tithing discussions by people who have literally not taken the time to inform themselves. I have heard so many theologians entering debates or posing questions in relation to tithing from your gross income or your net income (David A. Croteau 2011). If we are going to ignore what the tithe was, and that it had to be harvest or flocks from the supernatural increase of completely the Land of Israel only, furthermore could only be collected by the Levites at a grand total of 23.3%, then the debate concerning gross or net income becomes futile. The gross or net debate is an extension of a man-made philosophy that cannot be substantiated in scripture and, in view of the evidence of Malachi and Nehemiah, becomes nonsensical. The audience for this book are the born and bred Israelites, with the rebuke concentrated not on the people, but on the Aaronic Priests.

Strangers to Israel, whom the 3rd tithe could be issued to by the Levites, did not even qualify for paying tithes under the Levitical system. Even if they were converted to Israelites, they still couldn't pay them. (Lev. 27:34; Num.18:23-24; Deut. 12:5-6, 11: Heb. 7:5) (Kelly 2007 p 90) So what would make anyone think they can use the above evidence and verses to support the idea that any member of a church must pay a minimum legal standard of 10% of their financial income to the church they are attending? This is where rightly dividing the word of truth becomes very important. If ministers decide to pick and choose verses and weave them together to support a particular philosophy on giving, there is a clear problem. As discussed in a previous chapter, if you decide to follow the law, then you need to follow the whole law. This philosophy has one purpose and one purpose only, and that is the hope of financial gain, assuring the congregation that it is a commandment in order to establish a foundation flow of finances to sustain the church or ministry. This may be a functional financial principle; however not a Christian Doctrine! When you hear the words 'Test me now by this', relating to the tithe in Malachi, my overall suggestion would be to 'test scripture', and see what God actually had to say about it in context. The pie in the sky philosophy of 'testing God' and experiencing thereby an 'open heaven', is nothing more than a repetition of Deuteronomy 28:12, when an open heaven is contextualised as rain to sustain a food harvest:

[12']The LORD will open to you His good [(a])treasure, the heavens, to give the rain to your land in its season, and to bless all the work of your hand. You shall lend to many nations, but you shall not borrow'. **Deuteronomy 28:12**

To simplify what we as New Testament Christians are required to do is communicated aptly by Stendall:

'Under the Old Covenant we were to give tithes and offerings. Under the New Covenant we are to give ourselves. A relationship with God is HIS present to us; to give ourselves to HIM is our offering'. (Stendall 2013).

Based on the evidence presented in this chapter regarding the book of Malachi, much interest by tithe paying churches is concentrated on the word 'Storehouse'. Replacement theology would substitute like for like and suggest the key word 'Storehouse', is the church. This however does not go along with the rest of the teaching of the law, or take into account the regulations the storage of the tithe was governed by. The tithes were mostly stored by the Levites in the Levitical cities for their sustenance and the keeping of their families. It went to their abode (Chron 31:15-19, Neh 12:44,47).This does not virtually mean a modern day Church, as in a theocracy the storehouses would have been owned by the state. New Covenant Churches are not part of the state in general and mostly do not receive help with their groceries. The storehouse was there for the purpose of the storage of food, not present day money, although money was readily available during the time of the Old Covenant. Furthermore, tithe collecting churches keep most of the finances for the running of the church and might do little in the form of food programs for the rest of the community. Even if they did, it would be a fraction of the running costs of the ministry.

The Old Testament tithe for the sustenance of the Levitical Priesthood is uniquely different from the present day tithe that is being taught, as nowadays tithes are not collected for the priesthood of all believers, but only for those in actual leadership. Tithes are being reserved for the leadership of the church and running of a ministry or building.

No Old Testament principles are followed in respect of first fruits, firstborn, temple taxes or vow offerings, which forms a basis for a pick and choose philosophy merely deciding what works, or what is worth keeping, and rejecting what does not. The whole concept of gathering or handling money on the Sabbath is forbidden within Judaism, so if replacement theology decides to go like for like, it should do the same thing and avoid handling money on a Sunday. (Kelly 2007 p 110-111)

Clearly this brings a lot of what has been taught in churches since the popularity of tithing gained ground in the 1870s onwards into some confusion. New Testament principles and modern day giving, is set out in a completely different way compared with the Old Covenant. This is why it is important that we investigate what constitutes the New Covenant according to scripture and indeed when it actually started.

Tithing: Reviewing Scripture in Context

What do the Gospels say about Tithing?

We are now moving on to the New Testament and the New Covenant and what it has to say about Biblical giving. The Old Testament ends with the book of Malachi with the word 'curse'; similarly the book of Genesis finishes with the word 'Coffin'. The New Testament is the renewed and better covenant and built on better promises (Hebrews 7:22, 8:6).

²² by so much more Jesus has become a ⁽ᵃ⁾surety of a better covenant'. **Hebrews 7:22**

⁶ 'But now He has obtained a more excellent ministry, inasmuch as He is also Mediator of a better covenant, which was established on better promises'. **Hebrews 8:6**

We have 400 silent years where the prophets were silent and no longer wrote, then the incarnation as God becomes fully man, but still fully God in the person of Jesus. We have the 4 biographies of Jesus in Matthew, Mark, Luke and John. Four different books, written from different perspectives, aimed at different audiences. The Gospels do indeed have reference to tithing. The important question to ask in this instance, is to ascertain what constitutes the Old Testament and New Testament in literary writing, and when contextually in the timeline triggers the New Covenant. This forms a very important basis in analysing the Gospels, specifically with regard to the teaching of Jesus and whom he was talking to, dividing law from grace (Romans 6:14-15).

¹⁴ For sin shall not have dominion over you, for you are not under law but under grace'. **Romans 6:14-15**

So when did the New Covenant start? The New Covenant is being explained in the upper room by Jesus as he uses the

Passover to explain the New Covenant fulfilling scripture as himself as the Passover Lamb.

[28]'For this is My blood of the [a]new covenant, which is shed for many for the [b]remission of sins'. **Matthew 26:28**

If you know your Gospels well, this was when the betrayal at the kiss of Judas was near, virtually close to the END of the Gospels, not the beginning. The New Covenant comes into force contextually at the point of Jesus' death at Calvary.

[14]'how much more shall the blood of Christ, who through the eternal Spirit offered Himself without [a]spot to God, cleanse your conscience from dead works to serve the living God? [15]And for this reason He is the Mediator of the new covenant, by means of death, for the redemption of the transgressions under the first covenant, that those who are called may receive the promise of the eternal inheritance'. **Hebrews 9:14:17**

It is therefore important to realise that Jesus' entire ministry in the Gospels took place under the Old Covenant. For example, the rich young ruler in Matthew 19:16 wanted to know how to inherit eternal life. Interestingly enough, the whole of chapter 19 is about the law and the account of the rich young ruler has more to do with keeping the law, than giving possessions to the poor:

[16]'Now behold, one came and said to Him, "Good[a] Teacher, what good thing shall I do that I may have eternal life?"

[17]So He said to him, [a]"Why do you call Me good? [b]No one is good but One, that is, God. But if you want to enter into life, keep the commandments."

[18]He said to Him, "Which ones?"

Jesus said, "'You shall not murder,' 'You shall not commit adultery,' 'You shall not steal,' 'You shall not bear false witness,' [19] *'Honour your father and your mother,' and, 'You shall love your neighbour as yourself.' "*

[20] *The young man said to Him, "All these things I have kept* [a] *from my youth. What do I still lack?"*

[21] *Jesus said to him, "If you want to be perfect, go, sell what you have and give to the poor, and you will have treasure in heaven; and come, follow Me."*

[22] *But when the young man heard that saying, he went away sorrowful, for he had great possessions'.* **Matthew 19:16-22**

The moral of the account holds much for us still today, but in a New Covenant context, Jesus would have emphasised the necessity of believing in him to be granted eternal life, (Acts 16:31, 1 John 5:13) not following the rigorous law of keeping the 613 Mitzvoth to satisfy the law. Salvation under the New Covenant can't be earned, but is given as a gift (Hebrews 8:6). This free gift can only be manifest in our lives through the person of Jesus.

The Gospels, therefore, have to be contextually taken into account as under the Old Covenant. The Law is yet fully operational, as all aspects of the law are still in need of being kept. The sacrificial system is in full flow and all Jewish feasts, beliefs and customs are being celebrated as prescribed in the Old Testament. John the Baptist and Jesus would have been circumcised on the 8th day, nothing according to the law would have been missed out. Now you may be wondering why I am spending a lot of time making this point about the Gospels; but this is precisely it, as anything said about **tithing** in the Gospels is indeed the fulfilment and requirement of the law that Jesus himself is supporting. We have two specific instances in Matthew 23:23-26 and Luke 11:41-42 that makes this evidentially clear.

*[23] "Woe to you, scribes and Pharisees, hypocrites! For you pay **tithe** of mint and anise and cummin, and have neglected the weightier matters of the law: justice and mercy and faith. These you ought to have done, without leaving the others undone. [24] Blind guides, who strain out a gnat and swallow a camel!*

[25] "Woe to you, scribes and Pharisees, hypocrites! For you cleanse the outside of the cup and dish, but inside they are full of extortion and [a]self-indulgence. [26] Blind Pharisee, first cleanse the inside of the cup and dish, that the outside of them may be clean also". **Matthew 23:23-26**

[41] "But rather give alms of such things as ye have; and, behold, all things are clean unto you.

*[42] But woe unto you, Pharisees! for ye **tithe** mint and rue and all manner of herbs, and pass over judgment and the love of God: these ought ye to have done, and not to leave the other undone".* **Luke 11:41-42**

These verses will always be used by ministers who support the tithing philosophy that tithing in itself, is a New Testament/New Covenant principle, as Jesus talks about it in Matthew and Luke and is therefore applicable to us today. The first theological point that needs to be made here, as I have started off the chapter explaining; one must separate the idea of the literal Old Testament/ New Testament from the applied Old Covenant/ New Covenant! The New Covenant only comes into force at Calvary and the veil being torn in two. Everything recorded before the death of Jesus in the Gospels should be regarded as literary New Testament, but Old Covenant. The next point I would like to make from both the accounts in Matthew and Luke, is that there is no mention of money. The **tithe** in this respect for the Pharisees is something that is consumed by the body or for a better word, to flavour

74

food in the form of mint and all manner of herbs. The weightier point I would like to make, specifically regarding these verses, is shown within the key word itself: **'weightier'**! The weightier matters of the **law,** justice, mercy and faith, they had neglected. Again, we need to look carefully at the word **law,** furthermore the priorities Jesus is setting as to what is more important. The Pharisees who were the priestly elite in very important positions had managed to almost exempt themselves from tithing through the Oral law that was put into writing in the Talmud (not applicable to Christians). They merely tithed from the spices in their kitchens and gardens and in many ways behaved in a similar way as described by Malachi's rebuke of the priests in the Old Testament. Jesus was clearly not a fan of the Talmudic add-on regarding the Mitzvoth, much in the vein of the Sabbath being there for man and not man for the Sabbath (Mark 2:27-28).

The Pharisees made many accusations against Jesus, including using the power of Beelzebub to perform miracles, healing on the Sabbath and collecting food from the fields on the Sabbath. One thing, however, they did not do, and that was accuse Jesus of not tithing and they would have taken the opportunity if the Law had given them an opening to do so.

'At that time Jesus went through the grain fields on the Sabbath. And His disciples were hungry, and began to pluck heads of grain and to eat. [2] And when the Pharisees saw it, they said to Him, "Look, Your disciples are doing what is not lawful to do on the Sabbath!"

[3] But He said to them, "Have you not read what David did when he was hungry, he and those who were with him: [4] how he entered the house of God and ate the showbread which was not lawful for him to eat, nor for those who were with him, but only for the priests? [5] Or have you not read in the law that on the Sabbath the priests in the temple [a] profane the Sabbath,

and are blameless? [6] *Yet I say to you that in this place there is One greater than the temple.* [7] *But if you had known what this means, 'I desire mercy and not sacrifice,' you would not have condemned the guiltless.* [8] *For the Son of Man is Lord* [b] *even of the Sabbath."*

Healing on the Sabbath

[9] *Now when He had departed from there, He went into their synagogue.* [10] *And behold, there was a man who had a withered hand. And they asked Him, saying, "Is it lawful to heal on the Sabbath?"—that they might accuse Him.*

[11] *Then He said to them, "What man is there among you who has one sheep, and if it falls into a pit on the Sabbath, will not lay hold of it and lift it out?* [12] *Of how much more value then is a man than a sheep? Therefore it is lawful to do good on the Sabbath."* **Matthew 12:1-12**

Now you may ask yourself why this is relevant to tithing. The whole reason Jesus did not pay tithes, is the very reason he was allowed to glean from the fields with his disciples in accordance with Leviticus 19:10:

[10] *And you shall not glean your vineyard, nor shall you gather every grape of your vineyard; you shall leave them for the poor and the stranger: I am the LORD your God'.* **Leviticus 19.10**

Using any New Testament evidence to support tithing is contextually inaccurate. Furthermore, assuming that everyone qualified to tithe is also questionable. You could only tithe if you had vineyards, orchards and herds in the Holy land of Israel. The tithe was always from the increase that came supernaturally. People who performed any trades to earn a living did not qualify to give tithes. For example, carpenters, metalworkers, tentmakers and any other craft related profession that did not require the supernatural increase from the land of Israel in the form of food did not qualify. This is why Jesus did not qualify to pay tithes. Jesus would have given free will offerings and would also have paid the temple tax as a matter of courtesy! This was done in actual physical money. He explained the following about the temple tax to Peter:

'When they had come to [a] Capernaum, those who received the [b] temple tax came to Peter and said, "Does your Teacher not pay the temple tax?"

[25] He said, "Yes."

And when he had come into the house, Jesus anticipated him, saying, "What do you think, Simon? From whom do the kings of the earth take customs or taxes, from their sons or from strangers?"

[26] Peter said to Him, "From strangers."

Jesus said to him, "Then the sons are free. [27] Nevertheless, lest we offend them, go to the sea, cast in a hook, and take the fish that comes up first. And when you have opened its mouth, you will find a [c] piece of money; take that and give it to them for Me and you." **Matthew 17:24-27**

As we can gather from Jesus' tone, he was not a great fan of the temple tax. Furthermore, if we consider any of the evidence given in the Gospels already concerning the tithe, Jesus brings up the Pharisees and specifically their hypocrisy and self-righteousness whenever the word tithe is mentioned. Tithing was, however, essential during the Old Covenant which was still in full operation up until the crucifixion, but even then, Jesus ties the topic in with those who would rather give food, rather than change their hearts for the better. This is no more evident than in the Parable of the Pharisee and tax collector. The tax collectors were the most hated people in the Jewish community as they collected funds for the Roman occupiers. People would spit on the ground or cross on the other side of the street when coming across a traitor to Israel, yet Jesus paints a very different picture when comparing a tax collector with a Pharisee:

'Also He spoke this parable to some who trusted in themselves that they were righteous, and despised others: [10] "Two men went up to the temple to pray, one a Pharisee and the other a tax collector. [11] The Pharisee stood and prayed thus with himself, 'God, I thank You that I am not like other men—extortioners, unjust, adulterers, or even as this tax collector. [12] I fast twice a week; I give tithes of all that I possess.' [13] And the tax collector, standing afar off, would not so much as raise his eyes to heaven, but beat his breast, saying, 'God, be merciful to me a sinner!' [14] I tell you, this man went down to his house justified rather than the other; for everyone who exalts himself will be [a]humbled, and he who humbles himself will be exalted." **Luke 18:9-14**

With the Old Covenant still applicable during this time, Jesus moves the goal posts and ups the game concerning priorities. The Old Testament law was issued so the people of Israel could respond in obedience to God's will. However, Jesus transforms the law by focusing on the attitude of the heart. In other words, he made it more perfect. Even when focusing on the Ten Commandments Jesus took things a step further. To not commit murder; people were not to be angry. To avoid adultery, people were to refrain from lust. In the like for like case of the Pharisee and the tax collector, Jesus compares two figures who traditionally according to the religious views of the day would have been at opposite ends of the spectrum, yet it is the tax collector of all people who could have been chosen who comes out justified due to genuine repentance, rather than the Pharisee who fasts twice a week and tithes of all he possesses. The priority for Jesus is and will always be the attitude of the heart. When moving to the New Covenant itself, biblical giving completely moved away from the Old Covenant system which we will analyse in the next chapter.

Tithing: Reviewing Scripture in Context

Judaism: Do Jews still tithe today?

In Judaism today, when the word 'tithe', comes to the forefront after reading from the Tenakh, it is evident that it may generate some nostalgic discussions concerning the customs of the past. It is therefore clear that whether in Orthodox or Reform traditions, it is not practised today as a matter of a fixed law. The legal basis of giving within Judaism also shows levels of division, as many recognise as we have previously explored, that tithes were given in the form of harvest and livestock. Some have asserted that tithing should be financial (Tosafot Ta'anit 9a, Commentary on the Talmud), but nothing is clear cut and there is no established practice set out in law regarding giving to the synagogue in respect of the tithe. If the tithe is seen as a custom, and some interpret the law as a requirement to give, then any finances raised due to a person's conscience or feeling of obligation will be transferred to charity. Charity *(Maasser Kesafim)* is therefore not the synagogue.

For most Rabbis however, the law is interpreted the same way that has already been described in this book, as I have kept to the strict definition of the tithe as described in the Tenakh, avoiding any modern day interpretations which are selective in nature, deciding which customs to keep and others to avoid. Even in the modern day, the interpretation of the law by the Rabbis puts tithing only in the realms of the land of Israel. Farmers with produce outside the land of Israel are not obligated to tithe as a custom. The whole weight of the law is only also in effect if there is a majority of Jews living in the land of Israel. The temple mount is missing the Jewish temple itself, and the red heifer has not been sacrificed to meet the demand of the purification rites. This means that everyone today would suffer from something called corpse contamination. This would make the tithe of no effect. Israel no longer has a Levitical system of tithing, which was the very nature and purpose of the tithe. The tithe was for the upkeep of the priests and Levites. The State of Israel used to be a theocratic state that had incorporated this whole system in Government for the separation of the tithes. Please take note of the word tithes as a plural, also heavily pointed out in previous chapters in this book. Rabbis affirm that there were 3 tithes. First tithe *'ma'aser rishon'* (Levitical tithe), the second being the *'maser sheni'* (taken straight to Jerusalem) and the third tithe *'maser ani'*, which was the tri annual poor tithe. Rabbinic sources do not adhere strictly to what is in the Tenakh, which is heavily affected by the oral law (Talmud) serving as a commentary. There are some strict Jews who may donate a tenth of their income to charity called 'the money tithe', or 'wealth tax', *'maasser kesafim'*, but for the most part there is absolutely no clarity whether any form of tithe is a voluntary contribution rather than an obligation (Jacobs 1995). Can I also make it clear again, charity is not the synagogue!

The issue the Jews face today is the lack of a temple standing on the temple mount. Furthermore, no ordained Levites or priests poses a very big problem for the Jews to put the law of tithing into operation, even if they wanted to out of lack of funds! To simplify what is stated in the beginning of this chapter: A synagogue-attending Jew is therefore incapable of tithing and if they would try to do so, they would be violating the very law of God which would be classified as sin. How are you supposed to pay tithes without Levites? It is the absence of the temple, which puts a spanner in the works. However, should the temple be rebuilt with priests rebuilding the altars and following the sacred traditions, then every Jew with produce from the Land of Israel, inside Israel, would then be once more required to tithe. Worthy of noting, within those parameters only! These parameters also include the strict lineage of the tribe of Levi. In other words, this would have excluded Jesus, Peter, Paul and any other Jew who was not a member of this tribe. When the temple is rebuilt according to prophecy, then this whole sacrificial system would be rebooted, and lineages would have to be carefully studied to ascertain who would qualify to act as a Levite or Priest according to the family tree.

What we do know however, as a matter of certainty, is that financial giving within the synagogue is covered by a system of buying seats within a synagogue. This clearly does not represent a ten percent tithe system and in many cases for better seats, will go far beyond 10% of an annual income. The money by a family, where everyone has their set seat, goes straight to the synagogue and not a charitable donation (*Maasser kesafim)*. The synagogue is also not to be interpreted as the Levitical priesthood or Levite. If I were to compare this system with church, you may have had the unwelcoming experience of being told to move as you were sitting in someone's favourite seat, but in the case of the synagogue, these seats are bought and paid for.

Concluding from the above evidence, what makes the Christian church think they can adopt an Old Testament Law without the authority to do so? The temple mount needs to be cleansed by a red heifer. The temple was destroyed in 70Ad, with not even a stone standing on top of another and there is no Levitical priesthood officiating at the altar. The Jews know that, and it was their system that was in place to begin with. Orthodox Jews are very strict followers of the 613 Mitzvah, from circumcision to kosher food eating laws. Some Ultra-Orthodox Jews do not even mix with the gentiles, so it is clear there are many who follow the law according to every stroke of the pen. Tithing however, cannot be followed as they lack the means to do so!

Tithing: Reviewing Scripture in Context

Jesus Christ – Our New High Priest

As we have previously discussed in this book, there is a distinct lack of evidence regarding any mention of tithing in the New Testament or in regard to the New Covenant. The book of Hebrews, however, does mention the word a number of times. First, however, we need to look at the historical setting to put things in context. The book of Acts in chapters 15 and 21, talks of a struggle between Peter and Paul pertaining to the Jews and Gentiles and the book of Galatians also throws this up with the difficulty of circumcision and those not willing to associate with the uncircumcised or non-kosher eating or Sabbath-keeping folk. Paul really had his work cut out trying to unite the Jews who were following the law strictly and the Gentiles who at first were not considered worthy of receiving salvation.

So, we have two distinct groups of the faith many years after the crucifixion of Christ, some still following the Jewish festivals and going to the Temple and others whose faith alone was in Christ, whereby there would have been no justification in the law. For those still attending the Temple and all the Jewish customs, tithing may have been a procedure followed until the destruction of the temple in 70 AD by the Romans. Of course, after this catastrophic event, this would no longer have been possible. Perhaps the book of Hebrews is a further warning to make amends in keeping with Grace. Marrying this custom with the emerging church would also have raised many questions. The groups of Jews and Gentiles were to be brought under a new umbrella and that was the Church, as a body of believers in Christ.

The writer of Hebrews is addressing the book to the precise audience he is trying to convince, ie: the Jews! The Jews are still hanging on to their customs. Chapter 7 thus becomes very important as it is the only time tithing as a topic is mentioned in the New Covenant. At this point I also need to specify, that chapter 7 is not about tithing per se, but rather the importance of Jesus Christ and a better covenant. We can't have the tail wagging the dog on this one. This extract is not evidence for the need of a tithe paying church, but rather the King of Righteousness, the need for a New Priesthood, the greatness of that New High Priest and the advantages of a better covenant. It is also putting the Old Covenant to rest with all of its laws and statutes.

The King of Righteousness

7 For this ꞏMelchizedek, king of Salem, priest of the Most High God, who met Abraham returning from the slaughter of the kings and blessed him, ²to whom also Abraham gave a tenth part of all, first being translated "king of righteousness," and then also king of Salem, meaning "king of peace," ³ without father, without mother, without genealogy, having neither beginning of days nor end of life, but made like the Son of God, remains a priest continually.

*⁴Now consider how great this man was, to whom even the patriarch Abraham gave a tenth of the ꞏspoils. ⁵ And indeed ꞏthose who are of the sons of Levi, who receive the priesthood, have a commandment to receive **tithes** from the people **according to the law**, that is, from their brethren, though they have come from the loins of Abraham; ⁶but he whose genealogy is not derived from them received **tithes** from Abraham ꞏand blessed ꞏhim who had the promises. ⁷Now beyond all contradiction the lesser is blessed by the better. ⁸Here mortal men receive **tithes**, but there he receives them, ꞏof whom it is witnessed that he lives. ⁹Even Levi, who receives **tithes**, paid tithes through Abraham, so to speak, ¹⁰for he was still in the loins of his father when Melchizedek met him.*

Need for a New Priesthood

[11] [Therefore, if perfection were through the Levitical priesthood *(for under it the people received the law)*, what further need was there that another priest should rise according to the order of Melchizedek, and not be called according to the order of Aaron? [12] For the priesthood being changed, of necessity there is also a change of the law. [13] For He of whom these things are spoken belongs to another tribe, from which no man has [2]officiated at the altar.*

[14] For it is evident that [our Lord arose from [Judah, of which tribe Moses spoke nothing concerning [priesthood. [15] And it is yet far more evident if, in the likeness of Melchizedek, there arises another priest [16] who has come, not according to the law of a fleshly commandment, but according to the power of an endless life. [17] For [He testifies:*

[*"You are a priest forever
According to the order of Melchizedek."*

[18] For on the one hand there is an annulling of the former commandment because of [its weakness and unprofitableness, [19] for [the **law** made nothing [perfect; on the other hand, there is the bringing in of [a better hope, through which [we draw near to God.*

Greatness of the New Priest

[20] And inasmuch as He was not made priest without an oath [21] (for they have become priests without an oath, but He with an oath by Him who said to Him:*

[*"The LORD has sworn
And will not relent,
'You are a priest [forever
According to the order of Melchizedek' "),*

87

²² by so much more Jesus has become a ⁻surety of a ⁹better covenant.

²³ Also there were many priests, because they were prevented by death from continuing. ²⁴ But He, because He continues forever, has an unchangeable priesthood. ²⁵ Therefore He is also ⁿable to save ⁸to the uttermost those who come to God through Him, since He always lives ⁴to make intercession for them.

*²⁶ For such a High Priest was fitting for us, ⁻who is holy, ⁹harmless, undefiled, separate from sinners, ⁸and has become higher than the heavens; ²⁷ who does not need daily, as those high priests, to offer up sacrifices, first for His ⁰own sins and then for the people's, for this He did once for all when He offered up Himself. ²⁸ For the law appoints as high priests men who have weakness, but the word of the oath, which came after the **law**, appoints the Son who has been perfected forever.* **Hebrews 7:1-28**

It can be seen that the writer of Hebrews is using the book of Numbers, specifically chapter 18 in making comparisons between the Aaronic Priesthood that was supplied and maintained by the law of tithing, with the New Priesthood in the order of Melchizedek, namely Christ. This new high Priest is eternal and completely under the spirit of Grace. This book addressed to the Hebrews presents Christ as the person who can solve their theological dilemma in making the transition from Old Covenant to New. These better promises included better sacrifices in the form of praise and thanksgiving and of course a better system of giving under grace.

If we once again look at who Melchizedek was, he was a very great and respected man. He was a contemporary of the King of Sodom, therefore a pagan Gentile priest whom Abraham brought the spoils of war to in the form of a tithe, fitting with the ancient culture. Although it is stated that Melchizedek was as servant of the 'Most High God', there is nothing to suggest that this reference does not refer to the Pagan deity of the time. The God of Abraham most assuredly was not the deity worshipped by the occupants of Sodom. The King of Salem can typically be translated into the King of Peace, which is also a title appropriate for the Messiah. This does not mean that the writer of Hebrews is saying Melchizedek and Jesus are the same person or pre-incarnate Christ; he is making a comparison in the sense of the Old Testament foreshadowing the New. As Dr Kelly writes:

'The writer uses Melchizedek **'typically'**, not **'historically"**. (Kelly 2007 p 150)

We therefore have a building up of this character Melchizedek to be compared to Christ the High Priest, not comparing like for like in the form of a Christophany. Just the fact that there was no record of the lineage of Melchizedek did not mean that he randomly came from nowhere in a puff of smoke, it merely meant that the records of his birth or heritage were not readily available. Jewish record keeping was immaculate and had Melchizedek made an appearance during the times after Moses, then no one would have paid tithes to him, for the very reason that you had to be from the tribe of Levi to receive tithes or officiate at the altar. Melchizedek had the limitations of mortality as did Aaron, but Christ is our High Priest forever.

So, we can see that the person of Melchizedek is being typified as a type of Christ as opposed to a pre-incarnate Christ. Had this person in Genesis actually have been Christ, then it makes nonsense of the whole meaning of the account and God revealing himself to man through Abraham, thereby calling him out of his father's household. The tithing references in Hebrews 7 allows the Jews to understand the person of this High Priest before the Law of Moses and then afterwards. The tithing aspect puts into perspective the authority of the individual. But there is one greater than Melchizedek and the Aaronic Priesthood, and that is Jesus! Perfection could not be achieved through the law, but only through Christ indicating the limitations of the Old Covenant system and tithing. Complete obedience to the law and therefore achieving Godly perfection was not possible. The entire tithing system provided for the Levitical system, but did not create a perfect person. The Priesthood therefore with all its ordinances was in need of replacing. This replacement supersedes the law, and puts the law of tithing into no effect.

This moves the Aaronic priesthood under the Levitical system to a better system, which is the system that puts the believer in the position of the priest of their household. We were unable to draw near to God through the Levitical system, as that was formerly only possible for the Aaronic High Priest to do in the Temple (Heb 9:7). We can now approach God with confidence, because we are the Temple of the Holy Spirit! If the Levitical system is being undone, then so is the tithing system that sustains it. The system of Grace is beyond the law. This is where the concept of free will offerings starts taking shape. This entire text in Hebrews 7 is not written to affirm the practice of tithing sustaining the Aaronic Priesthood, but rather the abolition of it for something better. If we cut the verses short and paste some of them together, thereby creating links where there are none, then the flawed tithing law in the new covenant can be substantiated.

However, if we read chapter 7 in its entirety, we can see how the comparison and the context unfolds. It is clear that within Christ the limiting factors are removed. There is no justification by just giving a set percentage. Nothing pertaining to the Law is suitable to sustain the Church and the 5 fold ministry. The law in this context means nothing and Christ himself means everything. Sustaining the body of Christ is not up to the natural, it is dependent on the supernatural. Jesus is therefore not limited by this old institution that has forever been laid to rest. The new covenant does not enforce circumcision, keeping of the Sabbath, Kosher eating and the like, so why is it suggested tithing is inferred in the New Testament without evidence in scripture? Chapter 7 is not suggesting Melchizedek is the same person as Jesus historically and therefore he is pre-law and you must tithe to the Pastor to keep the church. Melchizedek and Levi are mentioned in order to do away with the old and to make a way for the new. Had all these ordinances not been abolished, including the tithe that sustained them, then we as the church would not be able to boldly approach the throne of Grace. It is the whole silence on the issue of tithing in the New Testament that lets us know that it had been laid to rest. Scripture is very specific in instructing us what to do and what not to do. Had a particular ordinance of the Old Testament been required, then the Epistles would have dealt with it. In Colossians 2:14 it is evident what Jesus did with these ordinances.

'Blotting out the handwriting of ordinances that was against us, which was contrary to us, and took it out of the way, nailing it to his cross'; **Colossians 2:14 NKJ**

Why some people choose to attempt to resurrect a system that was in place as if our Saviour had not finished his work is very questionable. The veil of the temple was torn in two, yet some with their actions are attempting to put it back, or for the very least, pretend that it never happened.

Tithing: Reviewing Scripture in Context

The Example of the Apostle Paul

Enter arguably one of the most hard working evangelists and teachers of the New Testament, the Apostle Paul. He worked more abundantly than them all (1 Corinthians 15:10). To set his credentials straight as to his authority, Paul makes the following statement to the Philippians:

'Circumcised on the eighth day, of the stock of Israel, of the tribe of Benjamin, a Hebrew of the Hebrews; concerning the law, a Pharisee'. **Philippians 3:5 NKJ**

Let us look at this verse and assess his credentials. The Pharisees along with the Sadducees ran the religious show of the time. Paul was so devoted to the law that he was willing at first to do anything for it, inclusive of killing Christians and looking after the cloaks of those who stoned the apostle Stephen in the book of Acts. His passion for the Old Covenant before his living revelation with Christ was going to take him to Damascus, whereby he could fulfil the mission given to him by the Sanhedrin, to wipe out the Christian population in the area or at least split up their families and send them into slavery. Here is a man who at first religiously could not have been further from Christ, yet on the road to Damascus had a life changing experience. After his living revelation of Christ, he was never going to be the same again. He in fact gained a higher revelation of Christ than Peter:

²" I know a man in Christ who fourteen years ago—whether in the body I do not know, or whether out of the body I do not know, God knows—such a one was caught up to the third heaven. ³And I know such a man—whether in the body or out of the body I do not know, God knows— ⁴how he was caught up into Paradise and heard inexpressible words, which it is not lawful for a man to utter'. **2 Corinthians 12:2-4 NKJ**

Without Paul, Christianity would have stayed largely with the Jews, following strict Kosher eating laws, keeping the Sabbath and circumcision as a sign of the covenant with God. Christianity would also have died out with the Jews at the time of the destruction of the temple in 70AD. In writing the epistles to various locations and people, he was the main contributor to the New Testament. To cut a long story short, he knew his stuff! If anything was a requirement in scripture, he would have referred to it and made it clear for all to see as he did not mince his words. Concerning those who were forcing the issue of the law regarding circumcision he wrote:

¹²As for those agitators, I wish they would go the whole way and emasculate themselves'! **Galatians 5:12** (NIV)

I don't think there are many scriptures that put things more bluntly concerning a requirement of the law being laid to rest. Now you may ask yourself why I feel the need to verify the credentials of Paul; after all his work speaks for itself. This is the precise point. Had there have been a requirement in the new covenant to **tithe**, let us be clear, he would have mentioned it! His blunt no-nonsense approach would have set the record straight! He would have gone into the Old Testament and foreshadowed it in the New Testament and made it a requirement and called it an eternal moral principle. Yet his silence on the issue is deafening. With all Paul endured in his sufferings, whether in persecution or lack of funds, would one not think that the person who wrote most of the New Testament would not have depended on his right to the tithe? Not once does he evoke anything relating to it in scripture or infer the need for it. He speaks of the need for support in the following scripture. However there is nothing pertaining to the tenth of a tenth or any relation to a percentage. Instead in 1 Corinthians 9: 1-19 we have a pattern of self-denial and the need to serve all men:

A Pattern of Self-Denial

9 'Am I not an apostle? Am I not free? Have I not seen Jesus Christ our Lord? Are you not my work in the Lord? ²If I am not an apostle to others, yet doubtless I am to you. For you are the ³seal of my apostleship in the Lord.

³My defense to those who examine me is this: 'Do we have no ⁴right to eat and drink? ⁵Do we have no right to take along ⁶a believing wife, as do also the other apostles, the brothers of the Lord, and Cephas? ⁶Or is it only Barnabas and I who have no right to refrain from working? ⁷Who ever goes to war at his own expense? Who plants a vineyard and does not eat of its fruit? Or who tends a flock and does not drink of the milk of the flock?

⁸Do I say these things as a mere man? Or does not the law say the same also? ⁹For it is written in the law of Moses, "You shall not muzzle an ox while it treads out the grain." Is it oxen God is concerned about? ¹⁰Or does He say it altogether for our sakes? For our sakes, no doubt, this is written, that he who plows should plow in hope, and he who threshes in hope should be partaker of his hope. ¹¹If we have sown spiritual things for you, is it a great thing if we reap your material things? ¹²If others are partakers of this right over you, are we not even more?

Nevertheless we have not used this right, but endure all things lest we hinder the gospel of Christ. ¹³Do you not know that those who minister the holy things eat of the things of the temple, and those who serve at the altar partake of the offerings of the altar? ¹⁴Even so the Lord has commanded that those who preach the gospel should live from the gospel.

¹⁵But I have used none of these things, nor have I written these things that it should be done so to me; for it would be better for me to die than that anyone should make my boasting void. ¹⁶For if I preach the gospel, I have nothing to boast of, for necessity is laid upon me; yes, woe is me if I do not preach the gospel! [17] *For if I do this willingly, I have a reward; but if against my will, I have been entrusted with a stewardship.* [18] *What is my reward then? That when I preach the gospel, I may present the gospel* [19] *of Christ without charge, that I may not abuse my authority in the gospel.*

Serving All Men

[19] *For though I am free from all men, I have made myself a servant to all, that I might win the more';* 1 **Corinthians 9:1-19** NKJ

All Jewish boys were trained in a particular skill from a young age to ensure they were able to earn a living wage. Although Paul was one of the very privileged and would have shown great intellectual promise and prowess from the start, he would have gained favour in the synagogue school compared with the other boys who would have gone straight off into their apprenticeship trades as carpenters, metal workers, masons, fishermen and other craft related professions. His theological studies would have been very much at the forefront, as he made it all the way to the Sanhedrin, yet the skill taught to him as a boy was that of a tentmaker. Paul was trained to be able to make tents out of goats' hair. This would have been his trade; furthermore the trade he relied on to keep him in ministry:

[3] *So, because he was of the same trade, he stayed with them and worked; for by occupation they were tentmakers'.* **Acts 18:3** NKJ

Assessing what Paul says in 1 Corinthians chapter 9, it is clear he was using his skill and trade to finance himself, with the occasional support from the church. He had to justify himself to the Corinthian church with Barnabas for the need of support; furthermore, feeling the need to make this request as an apostle who had had a living revelation of Christ. It is evident that in chapter 9 he is alluding to the fact that he is being accused by the church of requesting full-time support and sustenance from them, as the apostles from the church in Jerusalem had done. He is not standing upon his rights as an apostle to receive financial support, but he does make the point that other professions from soldiers, grape vine farmers and herdsmen receive certain benefits from their line of work. He makes it clear that he is well within his means to request right of support, yet his emphasis is not on a demand for sustenance, but rather being able to present the gospel without charge and not abusing his authority in the gospel. Paul is not negating full-time ministry by this, but in his case it is clear that for the most part he preferred to be self-sufficient. We also need to take into account why he was happy not to receive a salary for his work in the Gospel. The culture he grew up in expected everyone to be self-sufficient. A matter of fact, Paul in his trade was so effective, one of his primary desires was seemingly to look after others as a way of living the Gospel:

³³ I have coveted no one's silver or gold or apparel. ³⁴ Yes, you yourselves know that these hands have provided for my necessities, and for those who were with me. ³⁵ I have shown you in every way, by labouring like this, that you must support the weak. And remember the words of the Lord Jesus, that He said, 'It is more blessed to give than to receive.'" **Acts 20:33-35** NKJ

This indicates a stark contrast to the Gospel that is preached by many today, more in line with self-help and improvement, rather than ministering the Gospel to the poor. We have some leaders exacting a right to the tithe, or putting great emphasis on it, whereas they themselves perhaps lead an extremely opulent lifestyle with multiple accompaniments, not typical of average expectancy or mainstream experience.

If we, however, consider what Paul writes in his letter to Timothy, true Gospel values are not linked to the selfish or self-indulgent, who are interested in financial gain.

[5] and constant friction between people of corrupt mind, who have been robbed of the truth and who think that godliness is a means to financial gain'. 1 Timothy 6:5 (NIV)

As a matter of fact, you would be very hard pressed to find any scripture to support the idea that the Gospel can be used as a tool to launch a person into financial prosperity. We also need to consider the fact that if collections are referred to in scripture, whether due to famine or any kind of recent disaster, it does not generally infer that the support is going directly to a church, but rather to the poor and needy. Scripture does not indicate that we are not allowed to prosper; however, a portion of the increase is indeed for the Lord and as shown in the following quote was laid aside at the beginning of the week to support the saints in need, not the local church. An important point to add, this collection is not evidence that any type of tithing is scripture. Furthermore, depending on the translation of the Bible used, 'as he may prosper', may also be translated as 'in keeping with income'.

'Now concerning the collection for the saints, as I have given orders to the churches of Galatia, so you must do also: [2] On the first day of the week let each one of you lay something aside, storing up as he may prosper, that there be no collections when I come. [3] And when I come, whomever you approve by your letters I will send to bear your gift to Jerusalem.' 1 Corinthians 16: 1-3 NKJ

Something that cannot be ignored when reading scripture is Paul's unquestionable desire to bless people. Not being a burden to others, rather to practise the role of the parent providing for a child. He was indeed blessed by God, so much so that he was able to sustain others, happily spending on others and not necessarily being appreciated for it. This, however, was his communication of his love for the Church:

¹⁴Now for the third time I am ready to come to you. And I will not be burdensome to you; for I do not seek yours, but you. For the children ought not to lay up for the parents, but the parents for the children. ¹⁵And I will very gladly spend and be spent for your souls; though the more abundantly I love you, the less I am loved'. **2 Corinthians 12:14-15** NKJ

The Apostle Paul also places much emphasis on the things that count. The most important thing of course pertaining to Godliness, being therefore content in what we have, as we can take nothing from this world with us, except riches that we have stored up in heaven by being obedient to Christ.

⁶Now godliness with contentment is great gain. ⁷For we brought nothing into this world, ⁸and it is certain we can carry nothing out. ⁸And having food and clothing, with these we shall be content'. **1 Timothy 6:6-8** NKJ

We do not have any evidence in the New Testament of set percentages used for giving and certainly not clearly: not in any of the letters from Paul. Tithing from the very nature of its definition had a set percentage. It was the law. If you had orchards, vineyards, lands and livestock, this meant you. Yet there is no distinction or classification of any type in relation to this model in the new covenant. You only have the concept of free will giving which was a percentage in keeping with your income and more importantly what a person desired to give in their heart. I decided to use the NIV for this quote, which includes more emphasis negating compulsion.

⁷Each of you should give what you have decided in your heart to give, not reluctantly or under compulsion, for God loves a cheerful giver'. **2 Corinthians 9:7** (NIV)

This verse is really the crux of the matter concerning

household giving. Paul instructed the high priest of the household within the realms of the new covenant and the priesthood of all believers, to give in keeping with their income; furthermore, to give according to the heart. The heart has a percentage in mind according to the means which are available. You cannot attach any kind of tithe percentage to that. Tithe means tenth, and there can be no squabbling regarding that definition. I am not going to reiterate the other types of tithe that existed in the old covenant, but by this point you probably are getting the gist. The other thing that weighs heavily is the word 'reluctance'. You either give cheerfully or not at all. Tithing did not require a happy face with a giving spirit: it was the law and if the Jews were in the category to tithe had to give the set percentage. It was the law! Another very important key word not just to consider, but also to ponder on for a decent amount of time is the word 'compulsion'. Tithing was not a matter of compulsion, or feeling compulsion to do something – it was a legal requirement devoid of feeling. Paul is very clear with this and I would like you to think how many times you have sat in church feeling compulsion to give, because the person at the front was indicating that you have a requirement to do so, whether tithe or free will offering.

I am fully aware of a lot of older Christian literature out there in defence of tithing, as the church needs an income. RT Kendall writes the following:

'People asking about tithing are probably, just trying to figure out how to give less'. (RT, Kendall, Tithing: A call to Serious, Biblical giving (Grand Rapids: Zondervan, 1982), 58.

It is also not difficult to work out that buildings and clergy need funds for their upkeep, but if we look at the Biblical models of giving in the New Testament, demanding an Old Testament principle to fulfil this need is questionable. The theory on the need to tithe can therefore only be substantiated by the silence of the issue in scripture, therefore argued that it hasn't specifically been revoked and therefore is still applicable. This philosophy would be very difficult to substantiate, especially in view of all the evidence already brought forth in this book. The Apostle Paul had the credentials, did not mince his words, and set it out pretty straight. The Church in the United States as a whole survives on average by 3% giving on behalf of their congregants (David A. Croteau: Perspectives on Tithing, 2011). Might one suggest that a strategy of demanding a tithing system may not be the best way forward? Perhaps following the teachings of the Apostle Paul may indeed ensure better provision, especially in the view of serving under a better covenant with better promises under Grace by faith.

Tithing: Reviewing Scripture in Context

Fixed percentage or relative proportion?

It is the very nature of this title that effectively is the dividing factor between the Old and New Covenants and all the evidence from the Old Testament and New Testament we have already studied confirms this. This, however, does not leave all questions answered in respect of giving on behalf of the church. This gap does not go unnoticed in an increasing church culture of tithe payers and free will offering contributors.

I once heard a sermon by a minister who had done the maths and worked out that a low percentage of his church members tithed, whereas most preferred the New Testament principle of giving. It came as no surprise that the minister decided to reheat an old sermon from the previous year asking the congregation if they preferred the 10% of a tithe, or the 100% as outlined in the book of Acts. Moral of the story was: *'If you do not want to pay the legal requirement of the law at 10%, then you should pay the 100% outlined in the early church. Maybe it would have been better if you had kept with the tithe'.* It never ceases to amaze me how ministers when they feel they require the funds will indeed present a brand new narrative to either balance the books or hit a financial target. The latter was more likely. So, which are the scriptures that ask for possible 100% in the New Testament? Let us start with an account in Acts:

[40] *And with many other words he testified and exhorted them, saying, "Be saved from this [ll]perverse generation." [41] Then those who [lm]gladly received his word were baptized; and that day about three thousand souls were added to them. [42] And they continued steadfastly in the apostles' [lu]doctrine and fellowship, in the breaking of bread, and in prayers. [43] Then fear came upon every soul, and many wonders and signs were*

done through the apostles. [44] Now all who believed were together, and had all things in common, [45] and [a] sold their possessions and goods, and divided [b] them among all, as anyone had need.

[46] So continuing daily with one accord in the temple, and breaking bread from house to house, they ate their food with gladness and simplicity of heart, [47] praising God and having favour with all the people. And the Lord added [a] to the church daily those who were being saved'. **Acts 2: 40-47**

This scripture may get used frequently to suggest that one should give all one has ie: the full 100%. The NIV is more explicit in the translation suggesting that they also sold property *'They sold property and possessions to give to anyone who had need'.* The fellowship of the believers were strong and there is no question there were many who were in need, but putting the scripture in context – there is no established church building to maintain and it was not illegal to meet in the temple. Furthermore, they broke bread from house to house and God added to their number. This is not an example of early communism, but it was done out of unity with Christ's love reaching out to the body. A similar explanation takes place in Acts 4:32-37 when the early Christians shared all things:

[32] 'Now the multitude of those who believed were of one heart and one soul; neither did anyone say that any of the things he possessed was his own, but they had all things in common. [33] And with great power the apostles gave witness to the resurrection of the Lord Jesus. And great grace was upon them all. [34] Nor was there anyone among them who lacked; for all who were possessors of lands or houses sold them, and brought the proceeds of the things that were sold, [35] and laid them at the apostles' feet; and they distributed to each as anyone had need.

*And *Joses, who was also named Barnabas by the apostles (which is translated Son of *Encouragement), a Levite of the country of Cyprus, * having land, sold it, and brought the money and laid it at the apostles' feet'. Acts 4: 32-37*

We need to take into account that this followed Pentecost, and constituted the birth of the Church. The Church was in its infancy, thousands were being added to their number over a short period of time. New bonds were being made whilst the Church was being established. Although it wasn't illegal to meet up in the temple area, they still met in houses and very likely over a period of time kept things low key, especially when soon after a great persecution arose starting with the stoning of Stephen, and Saul pouring out his revenge upon those whom he considered heretics to the old covenant. Establishing the Church did require the people's needs being met.

At this point in time you may be wondering how these scriptures reflect on your levels of giving. Well, at first glance it is pretty convicting on behalf of providing for those in need. On closer inspection of the text, we discover that people who were possessors of Land(s) and house(s) sold them and laid the proceeds at the apostle's feet. This is speaking of a surplus or the rich taking care of the needy, so much so that there was no one left in need during a very difficult time following the birth of the church. Notice, the church is the body of Christ. The Church is the people. The Church is not a temple or lavish building! It was a community of believers, where no one was left in need. The practice of selling lands also throws up a very interesting account in Acts 5 with Ananais and Sapphira:

Lying to the Holy Spirit

*5 But a certain man named Ananias, with Sapphira his wife, sold a possession. *And he kept back part of the proceeds, his* *wife also being aware of it, and brought a certain part and laid it at the apostles' feet.* ³ *But Peter said, "Ananias, why has Satan filled your heart to lie to the Holy Spirit and keep back part of the price of the land for yourself?* ⁴ *While it remained, was it not your own? And after it was sold, was it not in your own control? Why have you conceived this thing in your heart? You have not lied to men but to God."*

⁵ *Then Ananias, hearing these words, fell down and breathed his last. So great fear came upon all those who heard these things.* ⁶ *And the young men arose and wrapped him up, carried him out, and buried him.*

⁷ *Now it was about three hours later when his wife came in, not knowing what had happened.* ⁸ *And Peter answered her, "Tell me whether you sold the land for so much?"*

She said, "Yes, for so much."

⁹ *Then Peter said to her, "How is it that you have agreed together to test the Spirit of the Lord? Look, the feet of those who have buried your husband are at the door, and they will carry you out."* ¹⁰ *Then immediately she fell down at his feet and breathed her last. And the young men came in and found her dead, and carrying her out, buried her by her husband.* ¹¹ *So great fear came upon all the church and upon all who heard these things.* **Acts 5: 1- 11**

You may have heard many sermons on this in regard to holding back what belongs to the Lord. Equally it may have been very much along the lines of the need of giving one's all, but also on close inspection of the text we discover that it is indeed about free will offerings and giving your best to God, and to be honest. Previously we discovered that the Apostle Paul outlined New Testament giving as a decision as to how much a person would decide to give per week. In the case of Ananias and Sapphira it was also a choice. They chose to sell the Land for an amount of money, but also decided to hold a percentage of it back, attempting to fool the apostle Peter. Peter was not fooled and neither was the Holy Spirit. Peter made it clear that the land was his and that he had full control over it, but both spouses decided to break an agreement and vow they had made to God and lied to the Holy Spirit and before men. If they would have been honest and said that they were giving the main portion to the Church, nothing would have happened. However, they decided to lie. Peter even gave the wife of Ananais a chance to redeem herself and tell the truth, but she continued the dishonesty she concocted with her husband. The young men carried her out also in the same manner of the departing of her husband. This is when something that one would suggest is a good deed, tips the scales and turns into a serious negative. The entire community were gripped with fear as a result. This is a lesson about free will giving. God does not require a percentage, he requires honesty. This wasn't even regarding equity or equality, it was all about reverently following through with a decision that was made based on a free will offering, not a percentage. The importance rests within honesty with God.

In view of the 100%, ministers may quite often use the example of the widows mite, which does indeed bring the question of relative proportions to the forefront:

The Widow's Two Mites

21 And He looked up and saw the rich putting their gifts into the treasury, ² and He saw also a certain poor widow putting in two mites.[a] ³ So He said, "Truly I say to you that this poor widow has put in more than all; ⁴ for all these out of their abundance have put in offerings [b] for God, but she out of her poverty put in all the livelihood that she had." **Luke 21: 1- 4 (NKJ)**

This account on the one hand has much to say about relative proportions of giving, but contextually does not imply that one must give 100%. The reason being? This verse is in the Gospels and the event happened during the Old Covenant as it was before Calvary. It was a free will offering, not a tithe! People could give free will offerings, but not everyone qualified to tithe food sources as you needed produce from land or flocks to do so. The context of what was going on would have been well understood by the people of the day and the hint is in the title of the extract. She was a widow! Tithes were for the poor, in particular the orphan, the **widow** and the stranger! She financially gave all she had into the treasury, with full knowledge that her needs were to be met by the same system she had just paid into! She was entitled as a widow to be looked after according to the law. Jesus knew this, but also knew that she had given all she had and explained the concept of relative proportion to the people. The tithe system worked for the poor in the Old Testament as it was correctly enforced, but in the new covenant it is no longer for the body of believers or the poor, but rather for the upkeep of a building and for the staff that work there. An important point to note at this stage – the Old Testament tithe was never used for the upkeep of the temple!

Considering relative proportion, it is difficult to ignore the Parable of the Rich Fool. Unfortunately, a lot of this wisdom we only hear taught in Sunday school:

Parable of the Rich Fool

[13] Then one from the crowd said to Him, "Teacher, tell my brother to divide the inheritance with me."

[14] But He said to him, ª "Man, who made Me a judge or an arbitrator over you?" [15] And He said to them, ª "Take heed and beware of ³covetousness, for one's life does not consist in the abundance of the things he possesses."

[16] Then He spoke a parable to them, saying: "The ground of a certain rich man yielded plentifully. [17] And he thought within himself, saying, 'What shall I do, since I have no room

to store my crops?"[18] So he said, 'I will do this: I will pull down my barns and build greater, and there I will store all my crops and my goods. [19] And I will say to my soul, [20] "Soul, you have many goods laid up for many years; take your ease; [a] eat, drink, and be merry." '[20] But God said to him, 'Fool! This night[t] your soul will be required of you; [s] then whose will those things be which you have provided?'*

[21] "So is he who lays up treasure for himself, [t] and is not rich toward God." **Luke 12: 13 – 21**

The first part of the parable is often ignored, although it seems to be the very reason why Jesus told the parable. A person from the crowd asked Jesus to use his authority to tell his brother to share the father's inheritance. According to the law it was the first born brother who inherited. Jesus is quick to not get involved, so much so that he refused to even comment on the situation, thereby not passing judgement. He does, however, tell the account of the rich fool, with the tearing down of old barns to make room for the plentiful harvest. Jesus is not criticizing a person receiving a plentiful harvest or the right to store harvest. However, he is making a very clear decisive point. Judgement will fall on those who lay riches up for themselves and are **not** rich towards God or others. There is a distinct possibility the man's workers in the field could have done with a raise. Furthermore, as this account is told during the old covenant, it is unlikely the rich fool was observing the gleaning law in Leviticus 19:9-10 and Deuteronomy 24: 19-22. We see the gleaning law actively in operation in the book of Ruth. The third tithe, being the tri-annual poor tithe was in operation when Jesus told this parable. This is something Jesus' audience would have understood well, as it was specifically for the widow, orphan and the stranger. There was no shortage of people like this experiencing almost absolute poverty and Jesus is addressing this need. The problem was not as much the storing up of wealth as much as it was **not** being rich towards God. It is the excess we have that we can give to the poor. The key verse to understand this parable is (verse 15). *[15]And He said to them, "Take heed and beware of[2]covetousness, for one's life does not consist in the abundance of the things he possesses."* The clear issue here is covetousness. This is an inordinate desire for possessions, whether your own, or the possessions of others. If your life simply consists of the desire to accumulate wealth, then you have clearly missed it, especially when you ignore the plight of your fellow man. Whatever we have done to the least of these, we have done unto Jesus (Matt 25:45).

One may ask how this reflects on our giving in church. Again, the key is to be honest with God. All I can do once more is echo what the Apostle Paul said to the Corinthians with no percentage attached:

[7]Each of you should give what you have decided in your heart to give, not reluctantly or under compulsion, for God loves a cheerful giver'. **2 Corinthians 9:7 (NIV)**

The dynamics of the church today have changed significantly. If you advocate today that you should be giving your all to the church, keeping nothing for yourself, then you would need to ascertain what constitutes giving to God. If the congregation you attend is by and large poor with little chance of rubbing their pennies together, yet the Pastor has a big house, expensive car and goes on lavish holidays, then you may need to spend some further reflection time. Equally, the pastor may be putting on a poor persona, but the public annual church accounts may indicate something very different. This is again where the word 'choice', becomes very important. We choose where we go to church. If we decide to attend a church with many paid staff and flashing disco lights during the service, then clearly we may need to adjust our 'free will' offerings accordingly. These places are not cheap to run and will offer you a particular flavour of Christianity. Others may prefer a more low-key church where the standard of giving will reflect the dynamics of the church. One thing to bear in mind is that the poor must not be ignored, neither the local community. The relative proportion debate also needs to balance your working week with your responsibilities at church. If you are already working in a caring profession that is taking up untold man hours, then you should not be put on the spot for doing insufficient work for the church. You are already being salt and light to the community. Your life is your ministry! God will hold us to account for what we have done all week and not just on Sunday or church related activities. In this respect it is important to remember that the most important and precious resource God has given us is 'time'. Money can be made and given away, but once time is gone it can never be replaced.

There is little chance of escaping the 'what would Jesus do?', scenario regarding giving. The only scenarios we have concerning Jesus' teaching on the matter are in the Gospels in the New Testament, but pre-Calvary, so therefore Old Covenant. The emphasis of giving one's all (100%) is no more prevalent than in the account of the Rich young Ruler, which is in three of the Gospels. It appears in the Gospel of Matthew 19:16-30, the Gospel of Mark 10:17-31 and the Gospel of Luke 18:18-30. We all know what the result of that was, as the young man walked away realising he could not give away everything his father slaved for. Not to forget as previously discussed in this book, the scriptures were in regard to keeping the law, not specifically instructions to the poor. This request, however, was typical for him as an individual and cannot be rolled out to the entire body of believers. How do I know that? If I contrast this account with Zacchaeus, then we see a different story:

19 *Then Jesus entered and passed through Jericho. ² Now behold, there was a man named Zacchaeus who was a* **chief tax collector, and he was rich.** *³ And he sought to see who Jesus*

*was, but could not because of the crowd, for he was of short
stature.* ⁴ *So he ran ahead and climbed up into a sycamore tree
to see Him, for He was going to pass that way.* ⁵ *And when
Jesus came to the place, He looked up* ⁽ᵃ⁾ *and saw him, and said
to him, "Zacchaeus,* ⁽ᵇ⁾ *make haste and come down, for today
I must stay at your house."* ⁶ *So he* ⁽ᶜ⁾ *made haste and came
down, and received Him joyfully.* ⁷ *But when they saw it, they
all* ⁽ᵈ⁾ *complained, saying, "He has gone to be a guest with a
man who is a sinner."*

⁸ *Then Zacchaeus stood and said to the Lord,* **"Look, Lord, I
give half of my goods to the poor; and if I have taken anything
from anyone by false accusation, I restore fourfold."**

⁹ **And Jesus said to him, "Today salvation has come to this
house, because he also is a son of Abraham;** ¹⁰ **for the Son of
Man has come to seek and to save that which was lost."** Luke
19:1-10 (NKJ)

Here we do not even have an ordinary tax collector, we have
a chief tax collector. He was so thrilled that Jesus was willing
to come to his house, he decided to give half of his goods to
the poor ie: 50%! Furthermore, we know that the money was
not earned in the same way as the Rich young ruler's Father,
as he had had to slave for the money. Zacchaeus was a person
who cheated people for a living. Yet Jesus affirms the 50%
with an extra bonus to those who were cheated, by suggesting
that salvation had come to his house that day. Jesus told the
Rich young Ruler who attempted to justify himself according
to the law, that he must give 100% to inherit the Kingdom of
God. The emphasis is, no one can obey the law entirely, no
one is good but our Father in heaven. Only Jesus can fulfil the
necessary requirement. To Zacchaeus's situation, Jesus
affirms 50% as salvation coming to his house. This shows us
that Jesus does look at our situation, our heart and decides
upon a particular requirement on our lives. We of course
need to be a willing participant. Not to forget, this is still Old

Covenant!

The title for this chapter is therefore misleading, as so many look upon the topic as an either/or scenario. The most important aspect of giving in the New Covenant is giving yourself as a living sacrifice. Jesus wants all of you! This does not require the percentage of a tithe. As far as financial giving is concerned, you give what you can when you can. It is unfortunate that some people have filled themselves with so much fear due to radical tithe teaching and are more likely to go into debt, not pay the rent or mortgage, or decide to skip meals to legalistically pay the 10% they believe is owed to God. If you are a minister making demand of the 10% tithe and the 100% principle being laid down at the apostle's feet, then you will need to ask yourself a number of questions. The Levitical tithe was for the poor (Levites and Levitical Priests who did not own land), the festival tithe was for the poor (yearly celebration with the Levites and Levitical priests) and the tri-annual poor tithe was of course for the poor, especially the widow, the orphan and the stranger. How much of this 10% does the minister give to the poor? If you are a minister leaning more towards the supposed new covenant giving of 100% at the apostle's feet, you would need to ask yourself the same question. How much of these finances laid down would be distributed as the accounts suggest to ensure there is no one amongst the body of Christ who is in need? Let us be honest within ourselves – it will mostly go for the upkeep of the church and church salaries in something we have gotten to know as corporate church. In many cases, a well-oiled machine intent on being run as a business, or at the very least something which is attempted to be built up as a mega church with a vision that is completely bound up in growth by numbers and bottoms on seats as a benchmark of success. The principle of giving obscene amounts of money to the church from experience is not for the purpose of the poor, except perhaps a well-advertised mission abroad. One doesn't usually tend to hear of the church paying off a person's car payment, mortgage, rent, household bills to ensure the congregation has their needs met, whereby wealth is distributed to anyone who is in need. You do, however, hear about wealth being demanded from the poor in the church with a promise of a financial curse if they do not give the full 10%.

Relative proportions throw up a very interesting fact. If a person is financially well off and follows the Old Testament legal tithe system in the new covenant, then just paying 10% of their income does not really make a big personal dent anywhere. If you are a low income household trying to balance the books and a legalistic tithe is demanded, it becomes a massive burden to balance the books and to try and stay out of ever-growing debt. In both these extremes it is not difficult to work out that according to relative proportion, some could be giving significantly more than the 10%, whereas others should be giving significantly less, or indeed be provided for by the church. When a person is struggling enough, the best the acquisitive church can do is tell them to give themselves out of debt, by increasing their offerings to the church, and that God can do more with the 90% than they can with the extra 10%. This is not common sense, it does not glorify God and it is stealing from the very poor people the Gospel (Good News) was for. Equally, as the high priest of one's own household, it is the family that should come first. As the apostle Paul writes to Timothy:

[8] But if anyone does not provide for his own, and especially for those of his household, he has denied the faith and is worse than an unbeliever'. 1 Timothy 5:8 (NKJ)

This is the type of verse that makes us stand back for a minute and decide upon the things that really matter. This was written at a time when sons may have been neglecting their widowed mothers and/or their immediate family at home and the rebuke is very clear concerning the neglect of the personal household. Love is expressed in action, and the denying of one's own, especially for those in a person's household was akin to the rejection of our Lord Jesus Christ: furthermore, being worse than an unbeliever. Most unbelievers look after their own! Why would people under the feeling of compulsion decide to do any different? After all, this was the body of Christ Paul was talking to, not the world. Frequently congregants are encouraged to give up all their savings, especially in corporate churches to finance the new church venture. Coming back to the needs of the immediate family aside from the Old Testament law, the book of Proverbs lets us know what a good father should do, even unto the second generation:

[22] A good man leaveth an inheritance to his children's children: and the wealth of the sinner is laid up for the just'. **Proverbs 13: 22 (KJV)**

When church leaders start moving away from the law of tithing, something else sometimes starts to creep in. Although finally claiming that tithing is the law, they then insist that under a better covenant with better promises that the 10% should thus be the starting point of giving, or for better words 'A minimum standard'. One can clearly see the motive behind this teaching, which also does not fall in line with any theological discussions in this book, neither in scripture. Our heart should be for the lost, yet in the New Testament Church, what we decide to do following God entrusting the newly converted to us, is to get them through foundation/discipleship classes and then demand 10% of their entire income. Might one say this pitch is not very attractive to a new convert, neither is it very successful. Equally, you may have prayed a lot for family members to be saved, or invited friends and neighbours to church, and following the possible positive noises your newly interested loved ones were making, you felt this sinking feeling. The sinking feeling was the full knowledge that at some point they were going to be asked for the 10% or even the same as a minimum standard. It is not particularly difficult to work out that this does not grow churches. This is especially common in corporate churches that do little for the community they are placed in and the financial contributions are quickly used up by this performance-driven mega machine. The mega churches or institutions that are aiming to be at this level mostly rely on mass migration of believers or sheep stealing to function, as large corporations are mainly set up for mostly seasoned believers educated or indoctrinated in giving.

If you are a church leader, can I encourage you to use the principles set down by the apostle Paul of free will offerings? We can preach all the sermons about Christ setting us free from the shackles, only to replace them with a new set of shackles rooted in legalism. This is everything Paul warned us about. Instead, could I encourage you to use God's standard of New Covenant giving? We can't go wrong if we use his divine principles. These divine principles worked when the Christian faith was spread by the 12 to become the largest world religion. If you trust in Him and put the new covenant to work, the financial needs of the body will be met by faith. There is no doubt that financial sowing can lead to financial reaping according to Paul, but the emphasis is not to receive, but to give:

[6] But this I say: He who sows sparingly will also reap sparingly, and he who sows [a]bountifully will also reap [b]bountifully. [7] So let each one give as he purposes in his heart, not grudgingly or of [c]necessity; for God loves a cheerful giver. [8] And God is able to make all grace abound toward you, that you, always having all sufficiency in all things, may have an abundance for every good work. [9] As it is

written:

"He has dispersed abroad,
He has given to the poor;
His righteousness endures forever."

[10] *Now* [d] *may He who supplies seed to the sower, and bread*
for food, [e] *supply and multiply the seed you have sown and*
increase the fruits of your righteousness, [11] *while you are*
enriched in everything for all liberality, which causes
thanksgiving through us to God. [12] *For the administration of*
this service not only supplies the needs of the saints, but also
is abounding through many thanksgivings to God, [13] *while,*
through the proof of this ministry, they glorify God for the
obedience of your confession to the gospel of Christ, and for
your liberal sharing with them and all men, [14] *and by their*
prayer for you, who long for you because of the exceeding
grace of God in you. [15] *Thanks be to God for His*
indescribable gift! **2 Corinthians 9:6-15 (NKJV)**

Tithing: Reviewing Scripture in Context

Church History: The Erosion of New Covenant Principles

I started this book with the quotes and objections by just a small number of church Fathers and theologians concerning tithing. The only New Covenant inference of tithing having taken place was the church in Jerusalem that continued to visit the temple, practise circumcision, honour the Sabbath, only physically consume kosher food or associate with those who practised the law. Yet this isn't evidenced, it is inferred. The Apostle Paul had much to say about this group of Jews who were not happy to mix with the Gentiles: therefore, it is likely they were doing everything to the letter of the law (Acts 15 and 21). This was explained in more detail in one of my previous chapters. This would have been brought to an end during the destruction of the temple in 70 AD. Other than this inference, there is no evidence of tithing taking place in the early church and every New Covenant principle and teaching of the Apostle Paul shows us that the statute of tithing was made obsolete. It is evidential that church leaders were self-sufficient, relying on trades taught them during their youth befitting Jewish culture. Every young man had to learn a trade and use his hands to earn a living. We do not have any evidence that Paul preached full-time earning a full-time wage as a result, except in possible missionary journeys, but it is clear that he shows hesitation in receiving any financial support. His trade of tent-making with goat's hair was the same trade taught to Barnabas. It is important to realise that Jewish Rabbis were not full time and did not collect a wage as this was not fitting with their culture. They worked to earn a living and taught in the synagogue.

We only have mention of tithing some 200 years after Calvary by some objections that St Irenaeus was raising. Who was Irenaeus? St Irenaeus (130 - 202) was born of Greek parents, leading Christian theologian of the 2nd century, Bishop of Lyon and clearly formulated church doctrine by which he took a strong stance against emerging Gnosticism, resisting all heresy and defining orthodox belief. He did much to validate both Testaments in the Bible during a time of confusion and upheaval (Encyclopedia Britannica). There is no mention of tithes from any Church writings or Fathers before him. Irenaeus wrote many sacred writings with untold volumes including 'Against Heresies' in the year 180 AD.

Concerning tithing in his book 'Against Heresies', he writes:

*"And for this reason did the Lord, instead of that [commandment], `You shall not commit adultery,' forbid even concupiscence; and instead of that which runs thus, `You shall not kill,' He prohibited anger; and instead of the law enjoining the giving of **tithes**, to share all our possessions with the poor; and not to love our neighbors only, but even our enemies; and not merely to be liberal givers and bestowers, but even that we should present a gratuitous gift to those who take away our goods"* **(Book 4 chapter 13)**

*"And the class of oblations in general has not been set aside; for there were both oblations there [among the Jews], and there are oblations here [among the Christians]. Sacrifices there were among the people; sacrifices there are, too, in the Church: but the species alone has been changed, inasmuch as the offering is now made, not by slaves, but by freemen. For the Lord is [ever] one and the same; but the character of a servile oblation is peculiar [to itself], as is also that of freemen, in order that, by the very oblations, the indication of liberty may be set forth. For with Him there is nothing purposeless, nor without signification, nor without design. And for this reason they (the Jews) had indeed the **tithes** of their goods consecrated to Him, but those who have received liberty set aside all their possessions for the Lord's purposes, bestowing*

joyfully and freely not the less valuable portions of their property, since they have the hope of better things [hereafter]; as that poor widow acted who cast all her living into the treasury of God'. **Irenaeus, Against Heresies, *Chapter 18. Concerning Sacrifices and Oblations, and Those Who Truly Offer Them,* 180 *AD***

Many church theologians support tithing, as the New Testament does not specifically state 'thou shalt not tithe', and therefore use the lack of evidence of the tithe to suggest that it must just have been a common occurrence and therefore not an issue. The absence of its mention in scripture and the erosion of new covenant principles in Church History and therefore its much later introduction by the Catholic Church is very telling! The Catholic Church would not have to introduce it, if it was common-place and part of established Christian Doctrine. There was no mention of tithing in the first council at Nicea 326 Ad, Constantinople in 381 AD, Chalcedon 451 AD, 2nd Constantinople 553 AD, 3rd Constantinople 681 AD, 2nd Nicea 787 AD, 4th Constantinople 869 AD or the Lateran Council in Rome in 1123 AD. (Kelly 2007)

Not all Bishops disagreed with the notion of tithing and Bishop Cyprian of Carthage is our first supporter for a possible move to this Old Testament system in the mid-3r^d century (Croteau 2015). He felt the clergy should possibly be fully supported in the same way as the Levites were sustained in the Old Covenant. Whether he was attempting to have it fully instituted or if he was making a simple comparison is unclear. Clarke points out that this attempt of introduction does also dispel the myth that tithing had been common place.

'This must imply that a strict system of tithing did not operate at the time in this area'. (Clarke 1984 p 157)

Cyprian therefore may have believed that 10% marks the minimum standard and a starting point for new covenant giving. This suggestion of course was only in North Africa, which was Bishop Cyprian's sphere of influence. Cyprian, however, did have conflicting views with many others in the Church, especially on his views on the papacy and who qualified to administer the sacraments. Cyprian would also not be popular amongst many tithe teachers today, as he encouraged bare necessities and giving all to the poor as opposed to enjoying the fruits of labour. This of course goes way beyond the tithe. He did, however, feel that the full time clergy should be supported by a tithe system.

When tithing was finally introduced it marked a time when New Covenant principles were being eroded. The introduction of the papacy and apostolic succession was a clear contrast to the principle of Priesthood of believers outlined in Hebrews. There was thus this new ruling class of clergy arising and a drastic change of theology. The order and structure of the clergy was closely resembling that of the High Priest, servants to the High Priest and common Levites for temple service. A higher caste system was put together and salvation was to be linked to the sacraments, with only specific people in the clergy allowed to administer them. The laity had been moved down to the bottom of the ladder! They would even need to go to the priest to be absolved of their sin in keeping with the High Priest in the Old Covenant. This was a picture of the watering down of the truth and doctrinal decline. Finally the introduction of tithing to the Catholic Church marked one of the final stages of moving away from the principles of grace and rather a devotion to law. This new law was the power and authority of the Catholic Church which considered the magisterium (Popes, Cardinals and Bishops) to have the final say. The writings of the magisterium were the authority of the Church and considered God's word, even superseding the Bible. The Catholic Church is built on a man

Peter, Cephas, 'the rock', (Matt 16:18-20) more so than the revelation that Peter had, that Jesus Christ was Lord and messiah:

¹⁵He said to them, "But who do you say that I am?"

¹⁶Simon Peter answered and said, "You are the Christ, the Son of the living God."

¹⁷Jesus answered and said to him, "Blessed are you, Simon Bar-Jonah, for flesh and blood has not revealed this to you, but My Father who is in heaven'. **Matthew 16:15-17 (NKJV)**

Unless the Lord builds the house, then the labourers labour in vain Psalm (127:1). Jesus affirms his authority and the rejection of the Religious by making this following statement quoting from Psalms 118:2:

⁴²Jesus said to them, "Have you never read in the Scriptures:

'The stone which the builders rejected has become the chief cornerstone. This was the LORD's doing, and it is marvelous in our eyes'? **Matthew 21:42 (NKJV)**

The erosion of New Covenant principles happened over periods of time to resemble the authority of man, and man's ideas. Man's ideas were reverting back to the notion that a large structure was the church. This large structure would have been buildings called Cathedrals, where the bishop would have his seat or throne. These structures required money to build, money to maintain, furthermore the upkeep of a full time clergy. The common phrase that the 'church is not the steeple, but the people', did not apply! The understanding of our body as the temples of the Holy Spirit and Priesthood of **all** believers (Hebrews 7:5,12,18) (Laity) had been completely eradicated. Paul writes:

¹⁹Or do you not know that your body is the temple of the

Holy Spirit who is in you, whom you have from God, and you are not your own? 1 **Corinthians 6:19 (NKJV)**

Historically, the tithe as a divine ordinance and merely an obligation of conscience only starts making a formal appearance legislated in the bishop's letters at the assembly of **Tours in 567** and the **Canons of the Council of Macon in 585.** The second Council of Macon also shows more tough talk on the issue as it was announced:

'Whosoever obstinately refuses it is forever excommunicated' (Croteau 2015).

This was of course based on Old Testament Priesthood. These Councils put tithing on regional church decrees, with excommunication of the body if not followed. It wasn't, however, civilly enforced until the Catholic Church had more political power so therefore difficult to fully control. The civil law enforcement then came into force between 774 – 777 during the reign of the Frankish King Charlemagne, whose sphere of influence also included northern Italy and Rome. The Pope at the time convinced Charlemagne to enforce agricultural tithing by quoting the **Mosaic Law.** Pope Hadrian attempted to institute a system of tithing on the Anglo-Saxons in 785. Moving on to 800 when Charlemagne was crowned the Holy Roman Emperor, the philosophy naturally gained much ground. Food tithing was introduced by King Edgar in England in 906. The Church Councils of Gerona 1067/1078 and the Fourth Lateral Council in 1215, meant tithing was rolled out to all Christian Countries. This system included tithing to the Church inclusive of non-practising Christians ie: The Jews. If there was ever an irony, forcing Jews to pay tithes as an Old Testament principle to the Church which should be a new covenant principle! One tenth to the Land ruler and the other tenth to the Church. The Crusaders, however, were exempted by the Third Lateran Council in 1179. The right of access to the tithes was also dependent on the ruling authority of the time. The right to collect tithes depended on who was more powerful, either the Church or State, but rest assured the tithes were collected. Pope Innocent 1198-1216 cemented the Church's power by legislating the importance of the Church over the State, therefore channelling the funds to strengthen its position. At this point if you are reading through the exhaustive dates of the councils and noticing the moral decay of the church establishment, I am sure you are beginning to view the word tithe and tax as synonymous. Based on the model of Israel's former theocracy! After a couple of centuries Jews decided to step further into banking, as the fine print allowed them to avoid paying tithes if they did not own land. This was forced upon them, as the right of ownership of land in many countries was under threat. There was much bitterness towards the papacy and not just by the Jews. In 1372 the clergy revolted against the pope, refusing to pay tithes to him. (Kelly 2007 p 260)

The Lutheran Theologian and botanist Otto Brunfels in 1524 did not make himself popular by the church establishment, claiming that the New Testament did not give room for tithing. This is not surprising, as Evangelical Protestants were continuously resisting the papacy. Brunfels as a botanist would have been fascinated with plants and the concept of reaping and sowing. He also knew the Old Testament tithe only related to food sources. If we consider the main separatists and leaders of the reformation there is a clear stepping away from religious tithing. Martin Luther and John Smyth concluded that tithing was not binding to Christians, Zwingli was left undecided and Calvin's utterances leant painfully towards the ambiguous (Croteau 2015).

The abolition of tithes in England was gaining ground between 1836 and 1850, mostly linked to moving away from Catholic principles. In the 1830s, tithes for church maintenance had become voluntary. The abolition of compulsory tithes only ended in 1871 in Ireland and 1887 in Italy. (Kelly 2007 p 261) Concerning the current situation in Germany I have written the Chapter 'tithing or taxation'? Germans increasingly are avoiding Church membership to escape the astronomical charges being brought to them for practising their faith. Europe by and large, however, has escaped this legalistic burden by the state.

From a current denominational point of view, expectation of tithing varies. I have never heard a Catholic specifically talking about 'the tithe', although it was introduced by the Catholic Church. One of the primary reasons the reformation gained so much popularity was because of the hate of the Papacy following the council of Trent, selling of indulgences for the purpose of freeing oneself and family members from purgatory. The hate for the tithe system of the day also fuelled this resistance. The original reformers correctly divided the word of truth and formally stepped away from this teaching. Most evangelical denominations include tithing in their church teaching and many use it as a pre-requisite to church membership. The Church of England, however, leaves the decision to the congregants.

This begs the question, why do Evangelical churches that claim to try and model themselves on the early church the best they can, resurrect this ancient practice? The reformation did so much to enable the common man to be able to read the Bible, and the power of the knowledge of God's word was once more in the hands of the people. Yet again, ever since especially 1870 the philosophy of tithing seems to have taken hold in the churches once again. People find it difficult to put ancient practices aside, so much so that while God had no problem getting the Hebrews out of Egypt, the people of their own choice could not let Egypt go.

Summary

You now will have undergone a very long contextual Biblical journey concerning the topic of tithing. This was also brought to you with careful historical analysis to ensure you knew about the audiences the scriptures were meant to capture and the way they would have culturally understood the word of God in their time frame. We established, that the early Church did not tithe. The Bible, Church Fathers, historical writers and theologians have confirmed this. Here is a condensed summary of the main points made in this book. In the last chapter I will condense these main points even further into bullet points as a theological/historical systematic review of evidence. This will allow a full overview of all scripture and context from historical sources to assist you to form your own opinion on the tithe as a Doctrine, and whether it has a place in new covenant teaching.

In our study of Abraham, we discovered that Melchizedek was a contemporary of the King of Sodom and was a priest who worshipped a pagan deity. He was not a pre-incarnate Christ. This is not a pre-law example of the eternal moral principle of tithing. Abraham followed the ancient Mesopotamian pagan practice of tithing a tenth in the form of spoils of war. Abraham went to war to recover his family and the goods from the King of Sodom. None of the goods were his! He deliberately decided to take nothing offered to him as a reward, except for what his men had already eaten. It is common sense to realise that you cannot tithe from something that is not your own. This is pre-law and the Levitical system had not yet been established. The Patriarch acted as High priest of the family.

In the case of Jacob, Abraham's grandson, the offer of the tithe to God was when Jacob was forced to abandon his father's household. We have no evidence of Isaac practising

127

it, and Jacob's vow to God was an act of desperation when he was running for his life. The Priestly Levitical system was still in his loins through one of his 12 sons, Levi. He had no one to tithe to; furthermore, there is no evidence he made good on his promise. This is not evidence of an eternal moral principle in operation to be resurrected by the New Covenant Church. The book of Genesis did not set tithing out as a command to follow.

The command to tithe is only found in the Mosaic Law. This was the law given to Moses starting with Aaron as the Levitical High Priest; however only started in the Promised Land. Tithes were **only** given in **food sources**. Land and flock owners could only tithe from produce from the Land of Israel. Any produce outside of the Land of Israel was not considered worthy. People only tithed if they had a harvest of grain, wheat, oil and wine. Herd owners tithed from their flocks and did not have to give the best of their flocks. The best of flocks was reserved for the Priests to tithe to the Lord! The only time the tithe was not food was in *(Deut. 14:25-27)*, if the tent of meeting for the festival tithe was too far, so the food items were sold, only to be re-bought at the destination of the tent of meeting and converted back into food. This enabled the people to celebrate with the Levites during the festival tithe once a year. The tithe was therefore **eaten** in the presence of the Lord! If you did not own land producing crops or herds producing cattle then you did not qualify to tithe! People who practised any trained crafts as was typical in Jewish culture for all males of a certain age did not tithe. Metal working, carpentry, tent making, or anything of the sort did not qualify a person to tithe. Fishermen also did not tithe as fish was not on a list of items you could tithe. You could only tithe from the supernatural increase of the Land of Israel. Non land or flock owners were entitled to give free will offerings to the temple treasury, if they so wished and during the time of the temple qualified to pay temple tax, but they did not tithe! Charitable arms could also be given.

There was not just one tithe as stipulated by all new Covenant ministers of the present day church, who vehemently try and collect them and suggest that replacement theology puts them in the present day position and authority of the Levites. This should not be a like for like theology! To collect tithe(s) plural, you had to be part of the tribe of Levi in Israel. Furthermore, not all Levites were priests. The tribe of Levi consisted of some who were priests; however, most Levites would be temple workers and would assist the priests in their duties. The upkeep of the temple required many workers on a shift system. The priests would officiate at the altar, whilst the Levites would fulfill all other duties associated with the temple from singing, to temple guarding and collection of tithes. Levites were not allowed to own land and therefore the tithe was there to sustain them through the Mosaic Law. Only the Levites could collect tithes. 10% went to the Levites who were allowed to take the food sources back to the Levitical cities for them and their families. 1% would go to the Priests who **ate** the tithe in the temple area. It is only the priests who had access to God in the holiest areas of the temple, anyone else would have lost their life if they would have tried. The people of Israel could only have their sin atoned through the High Priest.

18 Then the LORD said to Aaron: "You and your sons and your father's house with you shall bear the [a] iniquity related to the sanctuary, and you and your sons with you shall bear the iniquity associated with your priesthood. (Numbers 18:1)

There were specifically three tithes of **food sources**! Again, I need to stipulate that the word tithe in the Mosaic Law can only relate to food and there is nothing in scripture to tell us otherwise. These three tithes were:

The first tithe (Levitical tithe) The Levites were all from the tribe of Levi, some of which were Aaronic priests. The 10% would go to the Levites and 10% of this tithe would go to the priests. The priestly tithe had to stay in the store house and be eaten in the Temple area, whereas the rest of the tithe for the Levites could be carried off the temple site and be taken home to their families or to one of the 13 Levitical cities. And again, it could only come from the Holy Land of Israel.

[20] Then the LORD said to Aaron: "You shall have no inheritance in their land, nor shall you have any portion among them; I am your portion and your inheritance among the children of Israel.

[21] "Behold, I have given the children of Levi all the tithes in Israel as [a]an inheritance in return for the work which they perform, the work of the tabernacle of meeting. (**Numbers 18:20-21**)

The second tithe (Festival tithe) was the tithe that was brought directly to Jerusalem the Holy City. The Israelites who had produce from their land, orchards, vineyards and herds would take this tithe to Jerusalem once a year and it was almost in the form of a family holiday. This tithe was in support of the festivals and a portion was consumed with the Levites in celebration with the tither's entire family. It formed a time of festivity and celebration in the presence of the Lord.

[6] There you shall take your burnt offerings, your sacrifices, your tithes, the heave offerings of your hand, your vowed offerings, your freewill offerings, and the firstborn of your herds and flocks. [7] And there you shall eat before the LORD your God, and you shall rejoice in [a]all to which you have put your hand, you and your households, in which the LORD your God has blessed you. (**Deuteronomy 12:6-7**)

The third tithe (Tri annual poor tithe) was for whom the name actually suggests. It took place every 3 years. It wasn't just for the widow and the orphan, it was also for the stranger who was not originally from Israel. (Side note, strangers to Israel were not allowed to tithe) This tithe went to the place it was needed in Israel and not specifically the Holy city. We have therefore three distinctly different tithes.

[28] *"At the end of every third year you shall bring out the tithe of your produce of that year and store it up within your gates.* [29] *And the Levite, because he has no portion nor inheritance with you, and the stranger and the fatherless and the widow who are within your gates, may come and eat and be satisfied, that the LORD your God may bless you in all the work of your hand which you do.* (**Deuteronomy 14:28-29**)

[12] *"When you have finished laying aside all the tithe of your increase in the third year—the year of tithing—and have given it to the Levite, the stranger, the fatherless, and the widow, so that they may eat within your gates and be filled,* [13] *then you shall say before the LORD your God: 'I have removed the* [a]*holy tithe from my house, and also have given them to the Levite, the stranger, the fatherless, and the widow, according to all Your commandments which You have commanded me; I have not transgressed Your commandments, nor have I forgotten them'.* (**Deuteronomy 26:12-13**)

Bringing the whole tithes (plural) into the storehouse is clearly because there were three of them. Not just more than one person tithing. This also causes a discrepancy with the expectation to tithe merely 10%. The tithe consisted of 10% Levitical tithe, 10% Festival tithe and lastly the tri-annual poor tithe consisting of 3.3% every year. This was a yearly combined tithe of **23.3%**. Three tithes of which 2 are 10% a year and 1 every 3 years, culminating into 23.3% of income. Then tithing on every 7th year and 50th Jubilee year would also need to cease. So, no tithing took place on the 7th and 50th year so the land could recover and crop rotation could take place. Tithing churches today do not let you off from tithing on the

7th or 50th year!

First fruits were not a tithe! It was small enough to be collected by hand and put in a basket, or could consist of a sheaf of wheat from a field. They were to be collected by those who produced harvest and presented to the priest.

In the book of Judges, the people rejected God as their King and wanted a Monarch in keeping with the pagan tribes they were surrounded with. The ruling monarch then became the person to receive the all-important 1st tithe, which cannot be described as anything less than a tax. This unpopular move was enforced by King David and Solomon. When Israel was being re-established under Persian rule, there is a good chance the King of Persia would also have benefited from this, as he was the ruling monarch. If we review the tax system in Western governments, in general it also includes the Welfare State. If you are employed, the tax which is being deducted from your salary is already used to support the poor. Your giving is not starting from zero just because you attend Church! In Germany people are leaving the Church in droves as the Church tax is unaffordable and in many cases even denying the faith!

If you are a tithe-payer being faithful to the Mosaic Law and deciding to include the tithe in the New Covenant, then you need to realise that you would only be permitted to tithe food sources from the Land of Israel. This does not include money! Food banks are becoming common place in many churches, which is a good thing! If you are deciding to agree with replacement theology, ie: equating the Levites like for like with the church starting in the book of Acts, then you may also only tithe in food. Might one suggest that turning up with non-perishable item of food every Sunday at Church will raise a number of questions!? There is also a reminder attached to this, that you cannot obey parts of the law. You would have to fulfil all the law, comprising 613 Mitzvoth. The basics of this law would include, circumcision, kosher eating and Sabbath keeping. You cannot just pick and choose which ones you want to lay to rest and which ones to resurrect!

The behaviour of the people in charge in the temple was often a source of annoyance for God, as the Priests did not always do as they were told. Eli the High priest and his sons were punished during the time of the Judges due to bad leadership (Samuel 4) leading to the glory departing. This in the Old Testament, however, was not an unusual occurrence. The Priests in the last book of the Bible, Malachi, also behaved badly in regard to lazy worship and theft. Malachi is quite a short book and easy to read, yet most people are only familiar with the verses about tithing. The structure of the book is outlined as the following:

Malachi 2:1-9; Malachi criticizes the leaders for not teaching the Law.

Malachi 2:10-16; Malachi addresses the unequal yoking of inter-marriage with other tribes whilst, divorcing their own wives.

Malachi 3:6-12; Malachi expresses God's distaste for the way the priests are trying to rob God by stealing the tithes.

Malachi 3:8-11 are chiefly the only verses most congregants are aware of concerning tithing, as it promises untold blessing if followed and the release of the devourer if disobeyed.

⁸ Will a man rob God? Yet ye have robbed me. But ye say, Wherein have we robbed thee? In tithes and offerings.

⁹ Ye are cursed with a curse: for ye have robbed me, even this whole nation.

¹⁰ Bring ye all the tithes into the storehouse, that there may be meat in mine house, and prove me now herewith, saith the LORD of hosts, if I will not open you the windows of heaven, and pour you out a blessing, that there shall not be room enough to receive it.

[11] And I will rebuke the devourer for your sakes, and he shall not destroy the fruits of your ground; neither shall your vine cast her fruit before the time in the field, saith the LORD of hosts'. **Malachi 3:8-11 (KJV)**

The specific context to the most famous verses in Malachi about robbing God comes into play when we realise how the priests were behaving. The book of Nehemiah is set at the same time period as the book of Malachi and forms the basis of understanding the nature of what is going on. This is likely to be the true and actual context of the verses in relation to robbing God. The Priests who were entitled to 10% of the 10% were neglecting the Levites and robbing them of their portion. As a result, the temple had to be shut down, as the Levites decided to go to the fields to work them in order to feed themselves, neglecting their part time temple shifts. The High priest Eliashib and Tobiah the Ammonite (related to Eliashib by marriage) were certainly not living their lives in favour of Israel. Tobiah was in direct opposition to Nehemiah's restoration and rebuilding of the walls of Jerusalem and gained favour with Eliashib the High Priest, who leased the store-rooms of the Temple to him, thus allowing him to flourish bountifully in business. These store-rooms were of course for the tithes. Nehemiah gained permission from Artaxerxes of Persia to return to the newly constructed temple in Jerusalem and restore the correct order; furthermore returning the storehouse to its proper and holy use. This required the necessary ritualised cleansing to allow this to take place, and the ejecting of Tobiah the Ammonite from the area. This is explained in Nehemiah 13:4-12. As established previously, the Church is not the people of Israel. Furthermore, the rebuke concerning robbing God was not directed to the people of Israel, but the behaviour of the Levitical Priests themselves. This has no place in a Sunday sermon requiring New Testament giving. Even if you were to reject the historical context of the book of Nehemiah, you cannot brush aside the fact that the priests were being rebuked, not the people of Israel.

Tithe-paying ministers are quick to point out that the word tithe does indeed appear in the New Testament. This, however, does not take into account when the New Covenant started. It is therefore important to realise that Jesus' entire ministry in the Gospels took place under the Old Covenant. For example, the Rich young Ruler in Matthew 19:16 wanted to know how to inherit eternal life. Interestingly enough the whole of chapter 19 is about the law and the account of the Rich young Ruler has more to do with keeping the Law, than giving possessions to the poor. The moral of the account holds much for us still today, but in a New Covenant context, Jesus would have emphasised the necessity of believing in Him to be granted eternal life, (Acts 16:31, 1 John 5:13) not following the rigorous law of keeping the 613 Mitzvoth to satisfy the law. Salvation under the New Covenant can't be earned, but is given as a gift (Hebrews 8:6). This free gift can only be manifest in our lives through the person of Jesus.

The Gospels, therefore have to be contextually taken into account as under the Old Covenant. There are two instances when the word tithe is mentioned in the Gospels. The Law is yet fully operational, as all aspects of the law are still in need of being kept. The sacrificial system is in full flow and all Jewish feasts, beliefs and customs are being celebrated as prescribed in the Old Testament. John the Baptist and Jesus would have been circumcised on the 8th day, nothing according to the law would have been missed out. Now you may be wondering why I am spending a lot of time making this point about the Gospels; but this is precisely it, as anything said about **tithing** in the Gospels is indeed the fulfilment and requirement of the law that Jesus himself is supporting. We have two specific instances in Matthew 23:23-26 and Luke 11:41-42 that makes this evidentially clear.

[23] *"Woe to you, scribes and Pharisees, hypocrites! For you pay* **tithe** *of mint and anise and cummin, and have neglected the weightier matters of the law: justice and mercy and faith. These you ought to have done, without leaving the others undone.* [24] *Blind guides, who strain out a gnat and swallow a camel!*

[25] *"Woe to you, scribes and Pharisees, hypocrites! For you cleanse the outside of the cup and dish, but inside they are full of extortion and* [a]*self-indulgence.* [26] *Blind Pharisee, first cleanse the inside of the cup and dish, that the outside of them may be clean also'.* **Matthew 23:23-26**

[41] '*But rather give alms of such things as ye have; and, behold, all things are clean unto you.*

[42] *But woe unto you, Pharisees! for ye* **tithe** *mint and rue and all manner of herbs, and pass over judgment and the love of God: these ought ye to have done, and not to leave the other undone'.* **Luke 11:41-42**

These verses will always be used by ministers who support the tithing philosophy that tithing in itself, is a New Testament/New Covenant principle, as Jesus talks about it in Matthew and Luke and is therefore applicable to us today. The theological point that needs to be grasped here, is that one must separate the idea of the literal Old Testament/ New Testament from the applied Old Covenant/ New Covenant! The New Covenant only comes into force at Calvary and the veil being torn in two. Everything recorded before the death of Jesus in the Gospels should be regarded as literary New Testament, but Old Covenant. The next point I would like to make from both the accounts in Matthew and Luke is that there is no mention of money. The **tithe** in this respect for the Pharisees is something that is consumed by the body or for a better word, to flavour **food** in the form of mint and all manner of herbs. The weightier point I would like to make specifically regarding these verses is shown within the key word itself: **'weightier'**! The weightier matters of the **law,** justice, mercy and faith, they had neglected. Again, we need to look carefully at the word **law**; furthermore, the priorities Jesus is setting as to what is more important. The Pharisees who were the priestly elite in very important positions had managed to almost exempt themselves from tithing through the Oral law that was put into writing in the Talmud (Not applicable to Christians). They merely tithed from the spices in their kitchens and gardens and in many ways behaved in a similar way as described by Malachi's rebuke of the priests in the Old Testament. Jesus was clearly not a fan of the Talmudic add-on regarding the Mitzvoth, much in the vain of the Sabbath being there for man and not man for the Sabbath (Mark 2:27-28).

If we consider any of the evidence given in the Gospels already concerning the tithe, Jesus brings up the Pharisees and specifically their hypocrisy and self-righteousness whenever the word tithe is mentioned. Tithing was, however, essential during the Old Covenant which was still in full operation up until the crucifixion, but even then, Jesus ties the topic in with those who would rather give food, than change their hearts for the better. This is no more evident than in the Parable of the Pharisee and tax collector (Luke 18:9-14). The tax collectors were the most hated people in the Jewish community as they collected funds for the Roman occupiers. People would spit on the ground or cross on the other side of the street when coming across a traitor to Israel, yet Jesus paints a very different picture when comparing a Tax Collector with a Pharisee. With the Old Covenant still applicable during this time, Jesus moves the goal posts and ups the game concerning priorities. The Old Testament law was issued so the people of Israel could respond in obedience to God's will. However, Jesus transforms the law by focusing on the attitude of the heart. In other words, he made it more perfect. Even when focusing on the Ten Commandments Jesus took things a step further. To not commit murder; people were not to be angry. To avoid adultery; people were to refrain from lust. In the like for like case of the Pharisee and the tax collector, Jesus compares two figures who traditionally according to the religious views of the day would have been at opposite ends of the spectrum, yet it is the tax collector of all people who could have been chosen who comes out justified, due to genuine repentance, rather than the Pharisee who fasts twice a week and **tithes** of all he possesses. The priority for Jesus is and will always be the attitude of the heart.

This also of course raises another important question. Do Jews practising Judaism still tithe today? Even in the modern day, the interpretation of the law by the Rabbis puts tithing only in the realms of the land of Israel. Farmers with produce outside the land of Israel are not obligated to tithe as a custom. The whole weight of the law is only also in effect, if there is a majority of Jews living in the land of Israel. The temple mount is missing the Jewish temple itself, and the red heifer has not been sacrificed to meet the demand of the purification rites. This means that everyone today would suffer from something called corpse contamination. This would make the tithe of no effect. Israel no longer has a Levitical system of tithing which was the very nature and purpose of the tithe. The tithe was for the upkeep of the priests and Levites. The State of Israel used to be a theocratic state that had incorporated this whole system in Government for the separation of the tithes. Please take note of the word tithes as a plural, also heavily pointed out in this summary. Rabbis affirm that there were 3 tithes:

- First tithe *'ma'aser rishon'* (Levitical tithe)

- The second being the *'maser sheni* '(taken straight to Jerusalem)
- The third tithe *'maser ani'*, which was the tri annual poor tithe. (Jacobs 1995)

There are some strict Jews who may donate a tenth of their income to charity called 'the money tithe', or 'wealth tax', '*maasser kesafim*', but for the most part there is absolutely no clarity whether any form of tithe is a voluntary contribution rather than an obligation. Can I also make it clear once more, charity is not interpreted as giving to the synagogue!

There are a number of factors preventing tithing from being practised in Judaism. The issue the Jews face today is the lack of a temple standing on the temple mount. Furthermore, no ordained Levites or priests poses a very big problem for the Jews to put the law of tithing into operation. To simplify what is stated in this summary: A synagogue-attending Jew is therefore incapable of tithing and if they would try to do so, they would be violating the very law of God which would be classified as **sin**. How are you supposed to pay tithes without Levites? It is the absence of the temple, which puts a spanner in the works. However, should the temple be rebuilt with priests rebuilding the altars and following the sacred traditions, then every Jew with produce from the Land of Israel inside Israel would then be once more required to tithe. Worthy of noting, within those parameters only! These parameters also include the strict lineage of the tribe of Levi.

What we do know, however, as a matter of certainty, is that financial giving within the synagogue is covered by a system of buying seats within a synagogue. This clearly does not represent a ten percent tithe system and in many cases for better seats will go far beyond 10% of an annual income. This money is paid by a family where everyone has their set seat, goes straight to the synagogue and not a charitable donation (*Maasser kesafim*). The synagogue is also not to be interpreted as the Levitical priesthood or Levite. The temple mount needs to be cleansed by a red heifer: the temple was destroyed in 70Ad, with not even a stone standing on top of another and there is no Levitical priesthood officiating at the altar. The Jews know that, and it was their system that was in place to begin with. Orthodox Jews are very strict followers of the 613 Mitzvah, from circumcision to kosher food-eating laws. Some Ultra-Orthodox Jews do not even mix with the gentiles, so it is clear there are many who follow the law according to every stroke of the pen. Tithing, however, cannot be followed as they lack the means to do so!

The book of Hebrews was written to attract the precise audience pertaining to its name ie: The Jews! The book was proclaiming Jesus as the New High Priest! As we have previously discussed in this summary, there is a distinct lack of evidence regarding any mention of tithing in the New Testament or in regard to the New Covenant. The book of Hebrews, however, does mention the word a number of times. First, we need to look at the historical setting to put things in context. The book of Acts in chapters 15 and 21, talks of a struggle between Peter and Paul pertaining to the Jews and Gentiles, and the book of Galatians also throws this up with the difficulty of circumcision and those not willing to associate with the uncircumcised or non-kosher eating or Sabbath-keeping Jews. Paul really had his work cut out trying to unite the Jews who were following the law strictly and the Gentiles who at first were not considered worthy of receiving salvation. So we have two distinct groups of the faith many years after the crucifixion of Christ, some still following the Jewish festivals and going to the Temple and others whose faith alone was in Christ, whereby there would have been no justification in the law. For those still attending the Temple and all the Jewish customs, tithing may have been a procedure followed until the destruction of the temple in 70 AD by the Romans. Of course, after this catastrophic event, this would no longer have been possible. Perhaps the book of Hebrews is a further warning to make amends in keeping with Grace. Marrying this custom with the emerging church would also have raised many questions. The groups of Jews and Gentiles were to be brought under a new umbrella and that was the Church, as a body of believers in Christ.

The writer of Hebrews is addressing the book to the precise audience he is trying to convince. The Jews are still hanging on to their customs. Chapter 7 thus becomes very important as it is the only time tithing as a topic is mentioned in the New Covenant. At this point I also need to specify, that chapter 7 is not about tithing per se, but rather the importance of Jesus Christ and a better covenant. This extract is not evidence for the need of a tithe-paying church, but rather the King of Righteousness, the need for a New Priesthood, the greatness of that New High Priest and the advantages of a better covenant. It is also putting the Old Covenant to rest with all of its laws and statutes.

It can be seen that the writer of Hebrews is using the book of Numbers, specifically chapter 18 in making comparisons between the Aaronic Priesthood that was supplied and maintained by the law of tithing, with the New Priesthood in the order of Melchizedek, namely Christ. This new high Priest is eternal and completely under the spirit of Grace. This book addressed to the Hebrews presents Christ as the person who can solve their theological dilemma, in making the transition from Old Covenant to New. These better promises included better sacrifices in the form of praise and thanksgiving and of course a better system of giving under grace.

I would not normally include so much detail in a summary; however, as Hebrews is the only effectively New Covenant evidence of tithe being mentioned, I cannot cut corners on this one. Clarity regarding the book of Hebrews chapter 7 is essential. If we once again look at who Melchizedek was, he was a very great and respected man. He was a contemporary of the King of Sodom, therefore a pagan Gentile priest whom Abraham brought the spoils of war to in the form of a tithe, fitting with the ancient culture. Although it is stated that Melchizedek was servant of the 'Most High God', there is nothing to suggest that this reference does not refer to the Pagan deity of the time, likely to have been Baal. The God of Abraham most assuredly was not the deity worshipped by the occupants of Sodom. The King of Salem can typically be translated into the King of Peace, which is also a title appropriate for the Messiah. This does not mean that the writer of Hebrews is saying Melchizedek and Jesus are the same person or a pre-incarnate Christ: he is making a comparison in the sense of the Old Testament foreshadowing the New. As Dr Kelly writes: The writer uses Melchizedek 'typically', not 'historically'. (Kelly 2007 p 150) We therefore have a building up of this character Melchizedek to be compared to Christ the High Priest, not comparing like for like in the form of a Christophany. Just the fact that there was no record of the lineage of Melchizedek did not mean that he randomly came from nowhere, it merely meant that the records of his birth or heritage were not readily available. Jewish record keeping was immaculate and had Melchizedek made an appearance during the times after Moses, then no one would have paid tithes to him, for the very reason that you had to be from the tribe of Levi to receive tithes or officiate at the altar. Melchizedek had the limitations of mortality as did Aaron, but Christ is our High Priest forever. So we can see that the person of Melchizedek is being typified as a type of Christ as opposed to a pre-incarnate Christ. Had this person in Genesis actually been Christ, then it makes nonsense of the whole meaning of the account and God revealing himself to man through Abraham, thereby calling him out of his father's household.

The tithing references in Hebrews 7 allow the Jews to understand the person of this High Priest before the Law of Moses and then afterwards. The tithing aspect puts into perspective the authority of the individual. But there is one greater than Melchizedek and the Aaronic Priesthood, and his name is Jesus! Perfection could not be achieved through the law, but only through Christ, indicating the limitations of the Old Covenant system and tithing. Complete obedience to the law and therefore achieving Godly perfection was not possible. This was the very point Jesus was making to the Rich young Ruler. The entire tithing system provided for the Levitical system, but did not create a perfect person. The Priesthood therefore with all its ordinances was in need of replacing. This replacement supersedes the law, and puts the law of tithing into no effect. This moves the Aaronic priesthood under the Levitical system to a better system, which is the system that puts the believer in the position of the priest of their household. We were unable to draw near to God through the Levitical system, as that was formerly only possible for the Aaronic High Priest to do in the Temple (Heb 9:7). We can now approach God with confidence, because we are the Temple of the Holy Spirit! If the Levitical system is being undone, then so is the tithing system that sustains it. The system of Grace is beyond the law. This entire text in Hebrews 7 is not written to affirm the practice of tithing sustaining the Aaronic Priesthood, but rather the abolition of it for something better. If we read chapter 7 in its entirety, we can see how the comparison and the context unfolds. It is clear that within Christ the limiting factors are removed. There is no justification by just giving a set percentage. Nothing pertaining to the Law is suitable to sustain the Church and the 5 fold ministry. The law in this context means nothing and Christ himself means everything. Sustaining the body of Christ is not up to the natural, it is dependent on the supernatural. Jesus is therefore not limited by this old institution that has forever been laid to rest. The new covenant does not enforce circumcision, keeping of the Sabbath, Kosher eating and the like, so why is it suggested tithing is inferred in the New Testament without evidence in scripture? Melchizedek and Levi are mentioned in order to do away with the old and to make a way for the new. Had all these ordinances not been abolished including the tithe that sustained them, then we as the church would not be able to boldly approach the throne of Grace. It is the whole silence of the issue of tithing in the New Testament that lets us know that it had been laid to rest. Scripture is very specific in instructing us what to do and what not to do. Had a particular ordinance of the Old Testament been required, then the Epistles would have dealt with it. In Colossians 2:14 it is evident what Jesus did with these ordinances.

'Blotting out the handwriting of ordinances that was against us, which was contrary to us, and took it out of the way, nailing it to his cross'; **Colossians 2:14 NKJ**

Why some people choose to attempt to resurrect a system that was in place as if our Saviour had not finished his work is very questionable. The veil of the temple was torn in two, yet some with their actions are attempting to put it back. We cannot sew the veil of the temple back up and put God back into a box with a clear conscience.

New covenant principles of giving can only really be put into context by the person who wrote most of the New Testament epistles. The Apostle Paul! He worked more abundantly than them all (1 Corinthians 15:10). To set his credentials straight as to his authority, Paul makes the following statement to the Philippians:

'Circumcised on the eighth day, of the stock of Israel, of the tribe of Benjamin, a Hebrew of the Hebrews; concerning the law, a Pharisee'. **Philippians 3:5 NKJ**

The Pharisees along with the Sadducees ran the religious show of the time. Paul, a Pharisee was so devoted to the law that he was willing at first to do anything for it, inclusive of killing Christians and looking after the cloaks of those who stoned the apostle Stephen in the book of Acts. His passion for the Old Covenant before his living revelation with Christ was going to take him to Damascus, whereby he could fulfil the mission given to him by the Sanhedrin, to wipe out the Christian population in the area or at least split up their families and send them into slavery. Here is a man who at first religiously could not have been further from Christ, yet on the road to Damascus had a life-changing experience. After his living revelation of Christ, he was never going to be the same again. He in fact gained a higher revelation of Christ than Peter (2 Corinthians 12:2-4). Without Paul, Christianity would have stayed largely with the Jews, following strict Kosher eating laws, keeping the Sabbath and circumcision as a sign of the covenant with God. Christianity would also have died out with the Jews at the time of the destruction of the temple in 70AD. If anything was a requirement in scripture he would have referred to it and made it clear for all to see, as he did not mince his words. Concerning those who were forcing the issue of the law regarding circumcision he wrote:

¹²As for those agitators, I wish they would go the whole way and emasculate themselves'! **Galatians 5:12 (NIV)**

If you want clarity, look no further! I don't think there are many scriptures that put things more bluntly concerning a requirement of the law being laid to rest. Now you may ask yourself why I feel the need to verify the credentials of Paul, after all his work speaks for itself. This is the precise point. Had there have been a requirement in the new covenant to tithe, let us be clear, he would have mentioned it! His blunt no-nonsense approach would have set the record straight! He would have gone into the Old Testament and foreshadowed it in the New Testament and made it a requirement and called

it an eternal moral principle. Yet his silence on the issue is
deafening. With all Paul endured in his sufferings, whether in
persecution or lack of funds, would one not think that the
person who wrote most of the New Testament would not have
depended on his right to the tithe? Not once does he evoke
anything relating to it in scripture or infer the need for it. He
speaks of the need for support in 1 Corinthians 9:1-19.
However, there is nothing pertaining to the tenth of a tenth or
any relation to a percentage. Instead in 1 Corinthians 9: 1-19
we have a pattern of self-denial and the need to serve all men:

All Jewish boys were trained in a particular skill from a young
age to ensure they were able to earn a living wage. Paul had
the same trade as Barnabas in making tents with goat's hair
and was fully self-sufficient (Acts 18:3) Assessing what Paul
says in 1 Corinthians chapter 9, it is clear he was using his skill
and trade to finance himself, with the occasional support from
the church. He had to justify himself to the Corinthian church
with Barnabas for the need of support; furthermore, feeling
the need to make this request as an Apostle who had had a
living revelation of Christ. It is evident that in chapter 9 he is
alluding to the fact that he is being accused by the church of
requesting full-time support and sustenance from them, as the
apostles from the church in Jerusalem had done. He is not
standing upon his rights as an apostle to receive financial
support, but he does make the point, that other professions
from soldiers, to grape vine farmers and herdsmen received
certain benefits from their line of work. He makes it clear that
he is well within his means to request right of support, yet his
emphasis is not on a demand for sustenance, but rather being
able to present the gospel without charge and not abusing his
authority in the gospel. Paul is not negating full-time ministry
by this, but in his case, it is clear that for the most part he
preferred to be self-sufficient. We also need to take into
account why he was happy not to receive a salary for his work
in the Gospel. The culture he grew up in expected everyone

to be self-sufficient. A matter of fact, Paul in his trade was so effective, one of his primary desires was seemingly to look after others as a way of living the Gospel (Acts 20:33-35). This of course is a big contrast to the Gospel that is preached by many today, more in line with self-help and improvement, rather than ministering the Gospel to the poor. Today we have ministers demanding their right to the tithe. If we, however, consider what Paul writes in his epistle to Timothy, true Gospel values are not linked to corrupt people who are only interested in financial gain (1 Timothy 6:5).

As a matter of fact, you would be very hard pressed to find any scripture to support the idea that the Gospel can be used as a tool to launch a person into financial prosperity. We also need to consider the fact that if collections are referred to in scripture, whether due to famine or any kind of recent disaster, it does not generally infer that the support is going directly to a church, but rather to the poor and needy. Scripture does not indicate that we are not allowed to prosper; however, a portion of the increase is indeed for the Lord, as shown in 1 Corinthians 16: 1-3. Something was laid aside at the beginning of the week to support the Saints in need, not the local church. An important point to add, this collection is not evidence of any type of tithing in scripture. Furthermore, depending on the translation of the Bible used, 'as he may prosper', may also be translated as 'in keeping with income'. We do not have any evidence in the New Testament of set percentages used for giving and certainly, clearly not in any of the letters from Paul. Tithing from the very nature of its definition had a set percentage. It was the law. If you had orchards, vineyards, lands and livestock this meant you. Yet there is no distinction or classification of any type in relation to the model of tithing in the new covenant. You only have the concept of free-will giving which was a percentage in keeping with your income and more importantly what a person desired to give in their heart. I decided to use the NIV, for this quote includes more emphasis using the word compulsion.

"Each of you should give what you have decided in your heart to give, not reluctantly or under compulsion, for God loves a cheerful giver'. **2 Corinthians 9:7** (NIV)

This forms the very basis and nature of giving in the New Covenant. Paul instructed the high priest of the household within the realms of the new covenant and the priesthood of all believers, to give in keeping with their income; furthermore, to give according to the heart. The heart has a percentage in mind according to the means which are available. You cannot attach any kind of tithe percentage to that. Tithe means tenth, and there can be no squabbling regarding that definition. The other thing that weighs heavily is the word 'reluctance'. You either give cheerfully or not at all. Tithing did not require a happy face with a giving spirit, it was the law and if the Jews were in the category requiring the tithe, then they had to give the set percentage. It was the law! Another very important key word to digest is the word 'compulsion'. Tithing was not a matter of compulsion, or feeling compulsion to do something – it was a legal requirement devoid of feeling. Paul is very clear with this and I would like you to think how many times you have sat in church feeling compulsion to give, because the person at the front was indicating that you have a requirement to do so, whether tithe or free-will offering. The Apostle Paul had the credentials, did not mince his words and set it out pretty straight. Perhaps following the teachings of the Apostle Paul may indeed ensure for better provision, especially in view of serving under a better covenant with better promises under Grace by faith.

The Church loves to pull percentages out of the sky, especially if there are financial targets to be met, which leads us on to relative proportions. If you are required to give according to Paul in keeping with your income, then it is quite clear that Paul understood the concept of relative proportions well. Relative proportions throw up a very interesting fact. If a person is financially well off and follows the Old Testament legal tithe system in the new covenant, then just paying 10% of their income does not really make a big dent anywhere. If you are a low income household trying to balance the books and a legalistic tithe is demanded, it becomes a massive burden to balance the books and to try and stay out of ever growing debt. In both these extremes it is not difficult to work out that according to relative proportion, some should be giving significantly more than the 10%, whereas others should be giving significantly less, or indeed be provided for by the church. When a person is struggling enough, the best the church may do is tell them to give themselves out of debt, by increasing their offerings to the church, and that God can do more with the 90% than they can with the extra 10%. This is not common sense, it does not glorify God and it is stealing from the very poor people the Gospel (Good News) was for. Equally, as the high priest of one's own household, it is the family that should come first. As the apostle Paul writes to Timothy that neglecting one's own household is akin to denying the faith, making a person worse than an unbeliever (1 Timothy 5:8)! Most unbelievers look after their own! Why would people under the feeling of compulsion decide to do any differently? After all, this was the body of Christ Paul was talking to, not the world. The book of Proverbs even informs us that a good man leaves an inheritance even to his children's children (Proverbs 13:22).

The principle of the tithe is not always a financial cut off point, as more is often required. When church leaders start moving away from the law of tithing, something else sometimes starts to creep in. Although finally claiming that tithing is the law, they then insist that under a better covenant with better promises that the 10% should thus be the starting point of giving, or for better words 'A minimum standard'. One can clearly see the motive behind this teaching, which also does not fall in line with any theological discussions in this book, neither in scripture. Other ministers decide that instead of the tithe of 10%, the New Testament requires at least 100 %. The book of Acts will frequently be misquoted to encourage a congregant to give all their income and savings. In other words, the early believers placed in certain cases all they had at the Apostles feet. However, this does not take into account that it was for the redistribution of wealth amongst all those who were in need ie: 'The Poor'! This was done so that no one was left in need! The Church was and is still 'The body of Christ and People of God'! In Acts the Church was in its infancy and under persecution. Furthermore, there were no church buildings to maintain or ministers on the payroll. Unless the leadership want to supply all the needs of the congregation, this strategy has no scriptural basis! This is when the all-important background and context puts things into perspective. Plundering the congregation of all they have, based on Church history and Parables being taken out of context is not a pre-requisite for church growth. Congregants are not in sin if they are saving up for their retirement. Currently in the UK people will have to work till 67 years of age before they qualify for the pension they have paid into, even for those in jobs that require sound physical fitness and health. If you are a church leader, can I encourage you to use the principles set down by the apostle Paul of free-will offerings? We can preach all the sermons about Christ setting us free from the shackles, only to replace them with a new set of shackles rooted in legalism. This is everything Paul warned us about. Instead, could I encourage you to use God's standard of New Covenant giving? We can't go wrong if we use his divine principles. These divine principles worked when the Christian faith spread by the 12 to become the largest world religion. If you trust in him and put the new covenant to work for you, the financial needs of the body will be met by faith. Systems of control choke the life out of a congregation. Faith, hope and love will nurture a more positive environment.

This finally moves us on to the teachings of the Church, which in many respects were not based on sound doctrine, neither correctly dividing the word of truth. This book of course aligns itself to a more protestant stance. This formulates the yawning gap between exegesis and eisegesis. In exegesis study and analysis are required to come to an informed conclusion whereby the interpretations are formulated. Eisegesis is the exact opposite in that evidence is taken out of context with a list of presuppositions formulating conclusions to fit a particular view or stance that you already have. Any introduction in church teaching of the tithe system as a new covenant practice can only conform to the latter. The only New Covenant inference of tithing having taken place was the church in Jerusalem that continued to visit the temple, practise circumcision, honour the Sabbath, only physically consume kosher food or associate with those who practised the law. Yet this isn't evidenced, it is inferred. The Apostle Paul had much to say about this group of Jews who were not happy to mix with the Gentiles, therefore it is likely they were doing everything to the letter of the law (Acts 15 and 21). This would have been brought to an end during the destruction of the temple in 70 AD. Other than this inference, there is no evidence of tithing taking place in the early church and every New Covenant principle and teaching of the Apostle Paul shows us that the statute of tithing was made obsolete. His trade of tent-making with goat's hair was the same trade taught to Barnabas. It is important to realise that Jewish Rabbis were not full time and did not collect a wage as this was not fitting with their culture. They worked to earn a living and taught in the synagogue.

We only have mention of tithing some 200 years after Calvary by some objections that St Irenaeus was raising. Irenaeus wrote many sacred writings with untold volumes including **'Against Heresies' in the year 180 AD.** Concerning tithing he clearly divided the old covenant from the new and placed tithing within the law and giving possessions for the Lord's purposes as a form of liberty in Christ in keeping with a new system of giving.

There was no mention of tithing in the first council at Nicea 326 Ad, Constantinople in 381 AD, Chalcedon 451 AD, 2nd Constantinople 553 AD, 3rd Constantinople 681 AD, 2nd Nicea 787 AD, 4th Constantinople 869 AD or the Lateran Council in Rome in 1123 AD. (Kelly 2007)

Bishop Cyprian of Carthage is our first supporter for a possible move to this Old Testament system in the mid-3rd century (Croteau 2015). He was, however, unsuccessful in this and his views were only limited to his own sphere of influence. He felt the clergy should possibly be fully supported in the same way as the Levites were sustained in the Old Covenant. Whether he was attempting to have it fully instituted or if he was making a simple comparison is unclear. Clarke points out that this attempt of introduction does also dispel the myth that tithing had been common place. Cyprian was also an advocate of the tithe being the minimum standard of giving. (Clarke 1984 p 157). Cyprian, however, did have conflicting views with many others in the Church, especially on his views on the papacy and who qualified to administer the sacraments. This of course goes way beyond the tithe. He did, however, feel that the full time clergy should be supported by a tithe system. When tithing was finally introduced it marked a time when New Covenant principles were being eroded. The introduction of the papacy and apostolic succession was a clear contrast to the principle of Priesthood of believers outlined in Hebrews. There was thus this new ruling class of clergy arising and a drastic change of theology. The order and structure of the clergy was closely resembling that of the High

Priest, servants to the High Priest and common Levites for temple service. A higher caste system was put together and salvation was to be linked to the sacraments, with only specific people in the clergy allowed to administer them. The laity had been moved down to the bottom of the ladder! They would even need to go to the priest to be absolved of their sin in keeping with the High Priest in the Old Covenant. This was a picture of the watering down of the truth and doctrinal decline. Finally, the introduction of tithing to the Catholic Church marked one of the final stages of moving away from the principles of grace and rather a devotion to law. This new law was the power and authority of the Catholic Church which considered the magisterium (Popes, Cardinals and Bishops) to have the final say. The writings of the magisterium were the authority of the Church and considered God's word, even superseding the Bible. The Catholic Church is built on a man Peter, Cephas, 'the rock', (Matt 16:18-20) more so than the revelation that Peter had, that Jesus Christ was Lord and Messiah. The erosion of New Covenant principles happened over periods of time to resemble the authority of man, and man's ideas. Man's ideas were reverting back to the notion that a large structure was the church. This large structure would have been buildings called Cathedrals, where the bishop would have his seat or throne. These structures required money to build, money to maintain, furthermore the upkeep of a full time clergy. The understanding of our body as the temples of the Holy Spirit and Priesthood of all believers (Hebrews 7:5, 12, 18) (Laity) had been completely eradicated. Paul's writings make it clear that our body is the temple of the Holy Spirit who lives in us and that we in ourselves are not our own (1 Corinthians 6:19).

The tithe historically only makes a more formal appearance as a divine ordinance and merely an obligation of conscience and legislated in the bishop's letters at the assembly of Tours in 567 and the Canons of the Council of Macon in 585. This was of course based on Old Testament Priesthood. These Councils put tithing on regional church decrees, with excommunication of the body if not followed. It wasn't, however, civilly enforced until the Catholic Church had more political power so therefore difficult to fully control. The civil law enforcement then came into force between 774 - 777 during the reign of the Frankish King Charlemagne, whose sphere of influence also included northern Italy and Rome. The Pope at the time convinced Charlemagne to enforce agricultural tithing by quoting the Mosaic Law. If we look at the Catholic Church today, I can safely say that I have never heard a Catholic specifically talking about 'the tithe', although it was introduced by the Catholic Church. Some conservative Catholic Churches in Africa may, however, still practice this. One of the primary reasons the reformation gained so much popularity was because of the hate of the Papacy following the council of Trent, selling of indulgences for the purpose of freeing oneself and family members from purgatory. The hate for the tithe system of the day also fuelled this resistance. Martin Luther hated indulgences and was not a fan of the tithe system. The original reformers correctly divided the word of truth and formally stepped away from this teaching. Most Evangelical denominations include tithing in their church teaching and many use it as a pre-requisite to church membership. Why do Evangelical churches that claim to try and model themselves on the early church the best they can resurrect this ancient practice? The reformation did so much to enable the common man to be able to read the Bible and the power of the knowledge of God's word was once more in the hands of the people. Yet again, ever since especially 1870 the philosophy of tithing seems to have taken hold in the churches once more. Ironically, the practice of tithing can only be found in Evangelical churches and some other sub-sections of Christianity. Doctrinally speaking, paying tithes in the New Covenant makes as much sense as an evangelical attempting to gain access to God through the clergy, in other words – a priest officiating at the altar. This is in fact counter reformational and is not aligned with the system of the Priesthood of all believers!

Conclusions of Systematic Review

I started this book with a famous quote from Dr. Ben Witherington III:

"A Text without a context is just a pretext for what we want it to mean..." (*Witherington 2009 p* 41)

I would like you to consider this quote carefully in view of the journey you have taken, unlocking the Old and New Covenants. Taking from the summary, I will further condense the findings into a systematic review based on the Bible evidence and the historical contextual evidence. This will give you a complete overview of the topic to allow you to form your own opinion relating to the tithe.

Pre- Law

- Tithing means 'One tenth'. If it is not one tenth, then it is not a tithe.
- Tithing was an ancient Mesopotamian practice relating mainly to spoils of war.
- Abraham tithed to Melchizedek respecting this Pagan practice. The spoils of war were not his.
- Melchizedek worshipped a Pagan God and was a contemporary to the King of Sodom.
- Melchizedek was not a pre-incarnate Christ.
- Abraham's tithe of spoils of war was not from an eternal moral principle of giving.
- Isaac didn't tithe, but was prosperous.
- Jacob made a vow to tithe, but did not honor this promise as he had no one to tithe to, as the Levitical Priesthood was still in his loins.
- There is no such thing as a pre-law agricultural tithe and Genesis is a book of the law. Genesis does not outline a commandment to tithe.

Mosaic Law

- Tithing was only part of the Mosaic Law given to Moses.
- Tithing only started in the Promised Land, not in the 40 years in the desert.
- Tithes could only come from the Land of Israel.
- If you lived outside of Israel you could not tithe.
- Tithes were only in the form of food. Wheat, oil, wine and herds from the Land of Israel.
- Only people who owned agricultural land or herds in Israel could tithe.
- If a person worked any craft related trade, they did not qualify to tithe.
- Tithes were collected by the Levites to sustain them. The tribe of Levi had no land inheritance. Most Levites were temple workers and some were priests.
- There were three tithes. Levitical tithe, Festival tithe and Tri-annual poor tithe.
- The Priests received a 10th of the 10th of the Levitical tithe.
- All tithing ceased on the 7th and 50th year of Jubilee to allow the land to rest. It was useful for crop rotation. Tithing on these years would have been a sin.
- Tithes were never presented in the form of money. Tithes were always eaten.
- The three tithes culminated annually to 23.3% of crops and herds.

Taxation

- Tithing was a theocratic system.

- Tithing was for the poor. (Levites and Widows, Orphans and Strangers)
- Tithing sustained the Levitical system.
- In later stages Tithing was used as a form of tax and also payable to the Monarch, whether King David, Solomon or the ruling Pagan governance.
- God warned them of this extra burden when the Jews demanded a King like other pagan cultures.

Malachi

- Malachi was a prophet.
- Malachi is an Old Testament and Old Covenant book.
- Malachi is the last book in the Old Testament.
- Malachi is a prophetic book in the confines of the Mosaic Law.
- Malachi is a short book that is rarely read or understood, frequently quoted out of context from select verses. These select verses are usually only Malachi 3:8-11 (KJV).
- Malachi is likely to be contextualised by the book of Nehemiah.
- The book of Malachi is a rebuke to the priests for lazy worship.
- The book of Malachi is a rebuke to the priests for stealing the tithes from the Levitical workers, so no food was found in God's house. They were therefore robbing God.
- Robbing God of tithes for the Levitical workers brought a curse according to the Mosaic Law.
- In the book of Nehemiah the High Priest Eliashib is punished for robbing God when hiring out the storehouse to Tobiah the Ammonite for selfish gain. He therefore robbed the Levites of

their portion of the Tithe. There was thus no food in God's house. The Levites shut the temple as a result and went home to their Levitical cities to find food.

- The Rebuke was for the Levitical Priests only and not for the people of Israel.
- Obedience to the Law brought a blessing and an open heaven to bring rain on the crops in season for a successful food harvest.
- The rebuke is not meant for the Gentiles or the Church.

The Gospels

- The Gospels are New Testament, but Old Covenant.
- The Gospels only become New Covenant after Calvary.
- Any reference to the tithe by Jesus is in relation to the law, which is still at that time in full operation.
- In Matthew 23:23-26 and Luke 11:41-42 Jesus affirms the tithe of spices by the Pharisees. He, however, rebukes the Pharisees' hypocrisy, neglecting the weightier matters of the law: justice, mercy and faith.
- In Luke 18: 9-14 Jesus speaks a parable comparing a tax collector and a Pharisee. The tax collector humbled himself and went home justified, whereas the self-righteous Pharisee was not justified by Jesus, although he fasted twice a week and gave tithes of all he possessed. Jesus again is calling out their hypocrisy.
- Any mention of the tithe by Jesus in the Gospels is linked to hypocrisy of the Pharisees.

- Other accounts when Jesus addresses the topic of giving is to be interpreted under the Old Covenant.

- The account of the Rich young Ruler, is the emphasis that you have to obey 100% of the law to inherit the Kingdom of God. Jesus knows this is not possible. The emphasis is therefore that Jesus is the person to fulfil the law perfectly. (Matthew 19:16-30, Mark 10:17-31, Luke 18:18-30)

- In the story of Zacchaeus the Chief tax collector, Jesus affirms that giving 50% would result in salvation coming to his house. (Luke 19: 1-10)

- Jesus addressing relative proportions with the Widow and her mites culminated in her giving 100%, does not contextualise the fact that the temple treasury was also open to her to be kept as a widow according to the law. (Luke 21: 1- 4)

- The Parable of the Rich fool, does not take into account whether he was tithing or not as an agricultural land owner, as he would then have done as the law required. It was, however, a severe rebuke based on covetousness and complete neglect of the poor. (Luke 12:13-21)

Judaism

- Modern day Judaism affirms that there were three tithes. First tithe *'maaser rishon'* (Levitical tithe). The second being the *'maser sheni* '(taken straight to Jerusalem) The third tithe '*maser ani'*, which was the tri-annual poor tithe.

- There are some strict Jews who may donate a tenth of their income to Charity called 'the money tithe', or 'wealth tax', '*maasser kesafim*', but for the most part there is absolutely no clarity whether any form of tithe is a voluntary contribution rather than an obligation. Charity is not interpreted as giving to the synagogue.

- Tithing is not practised in Judaism, as you can only tithe to the tribe of Levi.
- It can only take place if most of the Jews are in Israel.
- Tithing could only happen from the produce of Israel and only by those with agricultural produce and herds.
- The Temple was destroyed in 70 AD, which put an end to the sacrificial system, so tithing cannot take place.
- The Temple mount would first have to be cleansed by the sacrifice of a red heifer for the Jewish temple to be rebuilt.
- A Jew attempting to tithe would be classified as sin.
- The synagogue is not financed by **maasser kesafim**.
- Synagogues are financed by families buying their seats. Everyone has their set seat. The more you pay, the better your seat.

Hebrews

- The only mention of tithing in a New Covenant setting is in Hebrews 7.
- Hebrews 7 is regarding the King of Righteousness, the need for a New High Priest and the Greatness of the New High Priest.
- The audience of Hebrews are the Jews, so the writer uses the Patriarch Abraham to present an analogy of a display of reverence to a mysterious Prince of Peace. The example of Melchizedek is used as a type of Christ.

- Hebrews mentions tithing when comparing Melchizedek to Jesus Christ.
- Hebrews 7 is about the New High Priest under a new covenant, not about tithing.
- The writer uses Melchizedek 'typically', not 'historically'.
- We have a building up of this character Melchizedek to be compared to Christ the High Priest, not comparing like for like in the form of a Christophany.
- Melchizedek is not a pre-incarnate Christ.
- Hebrews chapter 7 is not encouraging tithing, it is laying it to rest in favour of a better covenant.

Teachings of the Apostle Paul

- Originally called Saul, there would have been no other as devoted to the Law as Paul from the tribe of Benjamin.
- He was from the tribe of Benjamin, not the tribe of Levi and therefore would never have collected tithes.
- Rabbis were not paid for teaching in the synagogues.
- Paul had a higher revelation than Peter.
- There is no mention of the need to tithe anywhere in the new covenant.
- Paul was a missionary first to the Gentiles.
- Paul discouraged circumcision, kosher eating and strict Sabbath keeping and all aspects relating to the old covenant. This is what put him at odds with the Jews in Jerusalem.
- Paul relied on the trade of making tents out of goats' hair, sharing the same trade as Barnabas.

- Paul was completely self-sufficient and did not rely on the church to support him financially, except on missions. He was not happy about asking for support.
- If the tithe system were a new covenant statute, he would have used it to support a full-time ministry, especially as the person who wrote most of the New Testament.
- He knew the law like the back of his hand and was aware more than anyone else, that it was completely linked to the Levitical sacrificial system and the temple in Jerusalem.
- Paul taught a system of free-will offerings, setting aside a sum which one has decided upon in one's own heart: not giving under compulsion and to do so happily. (2 Corinthians 9:7)
- Deciding upon what to give does not match up with a percentage. This cannot mean 10%.

Church History

- There is no recorded evidence of tithing in the early church.
- We only have mention of tithing some 200 years after Calvary by some objections that St Irenaeus was raising. **Irenaeus wrote many sacred writings with untold volumes including 'Against Heresies' in the year 180 AD.**
- Bishop Cyprian of Carthage is our first supporter for a possible move to this Old Testament system in the mid-3rd century. He was, however, unsuccessful in this and his views were only limited to his own sphere of influence in Carthage, North Africa.

- When tithing was finally introduced it marked a time when New Covenant principles were being eroded.

- The introduction of the papacy and apostolic succession was a clear contrast to the principle of Priesthood of believers outlined in Hebrews. There was thus this new ruling class of clergy arising and a drastic change of theology.

- The order and structure of the clergy was closely resembling that of the High Priest, servants to the High Priest and common Levites for temple service.

- A higher caste system was put together and salvation was to be linked to the sacraments, with only specific people in the clergy allowed to administer them. The laity had been moved down to the bottom of the ladder.

- People now had to go to the priest to be absolved of their sin in keeping with the High Priest in the Old Covenant. This was a picture of the watering down of the truth and doctrinal decline.

- Finally the introduction of tithing to the Catholic Church marked one of the final stages of moving away from the principles of grace and rather a devotion to the Mosaic Law.

- The Catholic Church only manages to fully legislate civil law enforcement of the tithe 774 – 777 during the reign of the Frankish King Charlemagne, whose sphere of influence also included northern Italy and Rome. The Pope at the time convinced Charlemagne to enforce agricultural tithing by quoting the Mosaic Law.

- The reformation did much to undo this forced taxation.

- The Catholic Church by and large no longer practises or teaches tithing.

- Nowadays tithing is mainly practised by Evangelical churches that would not exist if it were not for the reformation.

Bibliography

Barker William, *The Adages of Erasmus 1946*, Translation by William Barker, University of Toronto Press, 2001

Bryan Alton, *The New Compass Bible Dictionary,* Zondervan Publishing House, 1974

Clarke G.W. *The Letters of St Cyprian of Carthage, Ancient Christian Writers 43,* Newman Press, 1984

Bulman Mary, *Social affairs Correspondent, Food bank use in UK reaches highest rate on record as benefits fail to cover basic costs,* Independent, 2018

Croteau David A, *Perspectives on Tithing, 4 Views,* B&H Group, 2011

Croteau David A, *You mean I don't have to tithe? A Deconstruction of Tithing and a Reconstruction of Post Tithe giving,* Pickwick Publications, 2015

Duignan Brian, *Encyclopedia Britannica,* 1989

Hodder and Stoughton, *Illustrated Bible Dictionary,* Thomas Nelson Publishers, 1986

Huggler Justin, *Compulsory income tax on Christians drives Germans away from Protestant and Catholic Churches,* The Telegraph, London 30th January 2015

Irenaeus, *Against Heresies, Chapter 18, Concerning*

Sacrifices and Oblations, and Those Who Truly Offer Them; 180 AD, Anonymous

Jacobs Louis, *The Jewish Religion: A Companion,* Oxford University Press, 1995

Josephus Flavious, Antiquities *of the Jews, iv. 240; Loeb ed. 93 AD*

Kelly Russell, *Should the Church Teach Tithing?* Writers Club Press, 2007

Kendall RT, *Tithing: A call to Serious, Biblical Giving,* Zondervan, 1982

KJV, *King James Bible.*

Luther Martin, *'How Christians should regard Moses',* August 27, 1525.

Meunier John, *Sermon 'The Use of Money'.* Methodist Publication. May 17th 2011

NIV, *New International Version Bible.*

NKJV, *New King James Bible.*

Spurgeon, Charles. *'Entry for 'Tithes',* Charles Spurgeon's Illustration Collection, 1870

Stendall Russell M, *The Truth About Tithing,* Life Sentence Publishing LLC, 2013

Talmud, *Bava Batra 15a*

Talmud, *Megillah 15a*

Talmud, *Megillah 17B*

Tosafot Ta'anit 9a, *Commentary on the Talmud*

Witherington Ben III, *The Indelible Image, The Theological and Ethical Thought World of the New Testament*, 2009

Wycliffe John, *Tracts and Treatises of John de Wycliffe, D.D. with Selections and Translations from his Manuscripts, and Latin Works.* Edited for the Wycliffe Society, with an Introductory Memoir, by the Rev. Robert Vaughan, D.D. London: Blackburn and Pardon, 1845

Tithing: Reviewing Scripture in Context

About the Author

Karsten Wille is married with two children and holds a B.A (Hons) in History and Languages, and Post Grads in Christian Ministry and Applied Theology. Karsten has worked as a Pentecostal Pastor, planting churches in the UK and working in a Missions and Evangelism department ministering the Gospel in Africa, Asia and South America. With a PGCE from Exeter University and studies with the Open University in Educational Research he has taught Religious Education in schools for 20 years with a keen interest in Apologetics. Karsten also speaks on Philosophy and Ethics at conferences and Bible Academies. He has contributed to Christian Radio for morning devotions and appeared on TV discussing the subject of Godly marriage.

CPSIA information can be obtained
at www.ICGtesting.com
Printed in the USA
LVHW040144151019
634128LV00008B/2657/P